BOOTH'S HANDBOOK

of

COCKTAILS

and

MIXED DRINKS

JOHN DOXAT

A PAN ORIGINAL

PAN BOOKS LTD : LONDON

First published 1966 by
PAN BOOKS LTD,
33 Tothill Street, London SW1

ISBN 0 330 10593 0

2nd Printing (revised) 1969
3rd Printing 1971
4th Printing 1973

Printed in Great Britain by Cox & Wyman Ltd,
London, Reading and Fakenham

Dedicated to the cause of omnibibulous Good Living and its adherents, and especially to she who has so vitally contributed to the field of mixed drinks, Miss June Ipper.

A new Anthology of Recipes, both simple and prodigious, collated to appeal to modern Taste; including various Information of a useful or curious Nature concerning some of the principal Spirits, Wines, Liqueurs and Beverages and the uses thereof; together with other matters pertinent to Drinks and Drinking; and also containing Advice and Opinions to beguile and instruct aspiring Bartenders, amateur and professional.

Contents

Contents   Page

Preface

THIS volume may be said to have had its genesis in the nineteen-thirties, when the Volstead Act had just been repealed in the USA and the Cocktail Age was in full swing in Britain. We then put out from Booth's 'An Anthology of Cocktails – together with selected observations by a distinguished gathering and diverse thoughts for great occasions.' (Reference is made to this now very rare publication in Chapter 2.) When, in 1965, my company achieved its 225th year in continuous business, thought was given to issuing a second edition of the Anthology, attuned to changed conditions. In due course, John Doxat, whom I had appointed our publicity controller, contacted Pan Books. This very important paperback publishing house evinced considerable enthusiasm for adding to their library an original on the subject of cocktails and mixed drinks, which, by its scope and price, would be something quite new in its field, and for which it was agreed there was an undoubted demand. Backed by the traditions and authority of my company, allied to the prestige and distributive organization of Pan, we felt confident of the success of this mutual venture. It was decided both to drop the somewhat archaic term Anthology and at the same time greatly broaden the book's interests. As managing director, I thought it best to give the author no brief, and though he has occasionally sought my advice he has tackled the task as if he were an entirely independent writer (and he

Booth's Handbook of Cocktails and Mixed Drinks

is pretty independent!). This is as it should be, but I feel I should emphasize the point he makes in his introduction that opinions expressed are his alone.

MICHAEL B. HENDERSON

The House of Booth's,
Clerkenwell Road, London, E.C.1.

'Venite Apotemus'

INTRODUCTION

Whys and Wherefores

MANKIND has drunk stimulants since the first accidental discovery that fermentation produces alcohol, and through the millennia has consumed spirituous beverages of varying sophistication, until reaching the refinements of manufacture and distillation of our own day when the production and sale of potable alcohol in all its forms are a vast item in international commerce and play a major part in the economy of many civilized lands.

Much may be said for total abstinence and more for temperance, yet, given free choice, a great majority of people will seek refreshment, solace, and even inspiration, in produce of press and still. No one would seek to coerce a person *to* drink; and all endeavours, however well-intended, by force of law to stop *from* drinking those who have acquired this habit have been doomed to failure and have usually heightened the abuses, real or imagined, they sought to cure. Evasion is rife, amongst those who can afford it, even in those countries where religion abhors alcohol.

There are those who for reasons physical or psychological should not imbibe, but do; and there are a few who literally succumb to alcohol. Perfectly true: these are problems not to be swept under the carpet, but tackled, personally, socially, and frankly, as increasingly they are being. However, it is no more practical to believe the problems connected with alcohol can be solved by prohibition or punitive taxation than to suggest the road toll can be abolished by banning the motor-car. Let us keep a sense of proportion; drunkards, or criminally stupid motorists, are a minute minority.

The great proportion of people sanely enjoys a drink of their choice, widely conditioned by regional preferences and budgetary considerations. The evening at the local pub; the friends in at the week-end; the diplomatic Cocktail party; even the business-lunch Dry Martinis – these are all connected with alcohol; are beneficial alike to social exchange, to oiling the wheels of commerce and – who knows? – to helping promote the comity of nations.

Our era has seen a marked growth in intelligent interest in wines and spirits; their consumption has greatly spread in quantity, variety, and distribution. As a corollary, a considerable literature has come into being for specialists and also to feed with information an entirely new public seeking advice and education about potables. Many a man who once would have confined his drinking to a crepuscular pint, and the woman who would formerly have occasionally sipped a glass of sherry-type wine, have been on holiday to Spain, have tried *retsina* in Athens . . . Numerous households have installed a bar in the sitting-room . . . However, when it comes to books there has been – 'til now! – an hiatus. There are splendidly comprehensive and expensive volumes of great authority. There are massive books of mixed drinks, bewildering in the sheer number of their recipes, but giving scant or no information about the constituent beverages. There are books about wine written by experts for experts, and at least one for beginners; yet these either ignore spirits or avoid recipes. There are semi-technical books in all price ranges. There are 'funny' books; cocktail booklets . . . the bibliography of alcohol is extensive indeed.

Yet it seemed to me, and the publishers concurred, that in all these tomes there was not one that, at reasonable cost and in entirely non-technical terms, outlined with impartiality the background to the leading drinks of the world, sensibly listed the drinks to be made from them, concisely explained certain apparently esoteric matters (proof, fluid ounces) that concern but confuse the average drinker, raised polemical questions for debate, and gave practical advice within the scope of the contents. I have endeavoured to fill this gap, at a sensible price.

I have not written for the expert or the pseudo-expert – though I anticipate such reading this in order, pedantically, to spot errors! I have written for the person of normal intelligence and curiosity, who enjoys gaining 'a little knowledge' (which is not half as dangerous a thing as no knowledge at all), who likes a drink with friends and family, and who, wishing to know more in detail on a specific aspect of potables, will turn up the appropriate reference. Thus, there is no place here for explaining techniques of distillation, the chemistry of fermentation; for words like congerics or ethyl-alcohol the initiated may seek in vain. I have tried to be ruled by commonsense. What would *I* like to know? has been my guiding principle. Therefore, this is truly a personal book: the opinions expressed, like any mistakes inadvertently committed, are wholly my own.

Proprietary brand names have been used where they are essential for explanatory purposes, or where, say, a mixed drink is peculiarly associated, by invention or tradition, with a particular brand; or where I find it pertinent to quote. At the conclusion I give acknowledgements for the various aid, collective and individual, intentional or involuntary, I have received during the happy task of compilation. I would here like to express gratitude to Miss Mary Wallis who heroically transcribed into neat typescript my first chaotic draft, without which help, as they say, this book could never have been finished.

JOHN DOXAT

At the Sign of The Red Lion,
Opposite the Clerk's Well,
near St John's Gate, London.

'I drink when there is an occasion, and sometimes when there is no occasion.'

Cervantes

CHAPTER 1

On The Buying of Drink

IT MIGHT seem unnecessary to give people any information on *how* to buy drinks. Surely they are capable, having the money, to go into an appropriate place and purchase, by tot or bottle, their requirements. Capable – yes. Yet, in Britain, purchasers often do fail to show good sense. Frankly, one has only to consider what a large proportion of bar customers simply ask for 'double whisky', 'two small gins', 'a brandy', or 'a sherry' without further specification. (Have *you* never done so? I don't mean where they know your likes and dislikes, but in a strange place.)

This was less important when the number of brands widely obtainable was smaller, when comparatively few specialized firms produced most of the popular drinks, and when, despite the foregoing, the retail and licensed catering trades were much more free (from ties and restrictions) than they are now. It is today quite possible for a brand of drink that many customers want, not to be readily available in a number of outlets in a given district.

The right to choose is a customer's privilege in non-totalitarian economy. That this right is sometimes being eroded is largely the customer's own fault – and usually his loss. Insistence by consumers on having the brand of drink they wish, at *all* times, must ensure that these brands are stocked. Any good retailer will want to please his customers, but why should he bother with those who show no discrimination?

A Note of Warning

While a bottle of liquor you buy for home consumption will be protected by some type of seal, you *may* have had the misfortune to be the victim of 'substitution' when purchasing by the tot. This illegal practice does exist and it would be naïve to ignore the fact.

If you believe you have been sold a measure of spirit, vermouth, sherry or port (the categories mostly affected), or anything else, which is not the brand you asked for – even if it came from a bottle bearing that brand's name – you should make this belief known by firm query or complaint to the highest quarter available to you. It's pointless to swear at the bar staff – and bad manners. But remember that your complaint – however good your palate – can only be an expression of opinion and you would be unwise to impute dishonesty. Yet you may, by a forceful declaration of your opinion, induce abandonment or discouragement of such 'substitution' if it *has* been practised.

Help the Trade Help You

The last offence of this nature which I remember coming to the Courts, related to famous brands of sherry and port. The prosecution alleged that bottles bearing these brands' names had been re-filled with British sherry and port 'type' wines. The defendant pleaded guilty, with a plea of mitigation claiming the fault lay with a dishonest employee, and was fairly heavily fined.

The proving of a 're-filling' charge presents technical difficulties, but now a remarkable new process has been perfected which will make it practically possible to identify with absolute clinical certainty the presence of ingredients alien to a particular brand. This will mean that legal proof of 're-

On the Buying of Drink

filling' may be established. This will be welcomed by the vast majority of all those involved in the liquor trade, for they are naturally concerned with its good name and also that they might unwittingly find their reputation tarnished through association with a dishonest underling. Doubtless, a few successful prosecutions by the appropriate authorities would greatly reduce the incidence of the obnoxious 're-filling' swindle.

The consumer is already heavily protected from the watering of drinks, and from the giving of short measure. If further teeth were given to those laws covering the illicit substitution of one brand for another, virtual total protection would be afforded to the public.

Name Your Choice

Number One rule in buying drink is always to specify by name the brand you prefer – even should it cost you a little more, in money or time. Insist on *your* brand and you risk no disappointment from an honest trader: you will gain credit as a person of discernment.

There is considerable variation in the taste, quality, and even strength, of different brands in the same category. For instance, sherries come in an immense range. Vermouth formulae have many shades of difference between rival makes. Whisky may be 'malty' or lighter-bodied; gin may be very dry, or dry and with more character, or more aromatic . . . The variations in spirits can be notably distinctive or extremely subtle, but each well-known brand has its own special character. Find the ones you like – and demand them. Insist – be fussy – get what you want . . . the State takes enough; you're at least left with a *choice*.

Local Supplier, Your Friend

By law, prices are now at the discretion of retailers. So, as everyone knows, in buying drinks one can look around for the most advantageous prices locally for one's preferred brands. However, 'most advantageous' doesn't necessarily mean 'lowest'. Your usual supplier may not be quite the cheapest in your area for your preferred brands, but he may be more conveniently placed – I have known of people spending ten shillings in petrol to 'save' five shillings on goods! – and he may offer advantages in other respects, like highly varied stocks, delivery, credit, collection of 'empties', and good advice.

The advice of a friendly and knowledgeable retailer is particularly to be looked for in buying drinks with which you are not familiar. You may want a certain type of wine say, for a guest, but it is not a type you happen to like yourself. Your retailer – or your wine and spirit merchant if you live on a grander scale – is the person to ask. If he knows his business, he will provide the best he has within the cost limit you set. You benefit by his knowledge; he gains your goodwill, and future business. With drinks, price is far from everything.

Rely on the Shipper

When it comes to buying wine, the other persons to get to know, albeit vicariously, are the shippers. Apart from the grandest wines bottled in their countries of origin, you will discover, by the hard but interesting process of trial and error, that the names of certain shippers and bottlers on a wine bottle mean a better wine of that type and at that price than those of others. For example, 'Beaujolais' (q.v.: Wines) can be rank bad and expensive under one shipper's name and excellent under others: the ordinary table wines you buy are usually a blend.

There is a great deal more to buying drink than plonking

down your money and asking for a bottle, or tot, of gin or whisky, a bottle of sherry, a bottle of red wine ... Without denigration of some excellent but little heralded brands, one can say that your sheer guarantee in spirits lies in the names and cherished prestige of those established brands that are household words; in aperitifs, liqueurs, fortified wines – and don't let us forget beers and squashes and mineral waters – the situation is much the same; in table wines, it is primarily the shipper on whom you must rely.

In the long run it pays to buy the best; the best is usually the best-value as well. Know your brand – insist on it. *You* are the consumer.

'Candy is dandy but liquor is quicker.'
Ogden Nash

CHAPTER 2

Cocktails – Fact and Fancy

NO ONE *knows* how the word Cocktail came to be associated
with special types of mixed drinks. Of the literally millions of
regular drinkers of Cocktails, comparatively few have probably even given a thought to the origin of this peculiar
word: those who have looked into the esoterically intriguing
subject must choose between what can only be unproved rival
theories.

Let us start with at least one fact. It was in 1806, in an
American journal called *The Balance*, that a Cocktail was first
described in print, in recognizable modern form, as 'a stimulating liquor, composed of spirits of any sort, sugar, water
and bitters.' As a mixed drink, Cocktail is mentioned in *Tom
Brown's Schooldays* and Thackeray's *The Newcomes*.

It is probable that the first true 'Cocktail Book' was *The
Bon Vivant's Guide, or How to Mix Drinks*, published in the
1860s by the American bartender Jerry Thomas, who, seeking
recipes, toured Europe with one thousand pounds' worth of
sterling silver utensils. He knew not the cocktail shaker but
used 'bar glasses' – which we would call mixing glasses. So
did Harry Johnson, self-styled 'publisher and professional
bartender', who in 1882 put out in New York his illustrated
*Bartenders' Manual, or How to Mix Drinks of the Present
Style*. This surprisingly modern work refers to numerous
Cocktails and (edition of 1900 in my possession) may contain
the first printed recipe for a Manhattan. One of Johnson's

illustrations shows an ice-filled bar glass with an inverted metal cone, whence obviously evolved the cocktail-shaker, and he thoroughly disproves the popular idea that Cocktails came in only with the Cocktail Age and Prohibition (q.v.).

A Sporting Chance?

Johnson also lists a 'bottle of Cocktail for parties'. Indeed, until shortly before his era Cocktails were mainly bottled drinks, taken in the morning – or drunk *al fresco* at sporting occasions. A sporting association may be one clue to the mysterious term. In the 18th century, 'Cock-ale' was a spirituous mixture fed to fighting-cocks in training, and spectators would sometimes use a similar concoction in which to drink the health of the cock with the most feathers left in its tail after a contest, the number of ingredients being the same as the number of feathers.

Let us consider other notions. One is that a chemist in New Orleans used to entertain his friends with a potion based on the ingredients previously quoted from *The Balance*. For some obscure reason he served this drink in double-ended egg-cups which, being of French extraction, he naturally called *coquetiers*. Americans amongst his acquaintance called these 'cockters'; hence 'cocktail'.

But this theory is certainly no more far-fetched than a similar French derivation, from *coquetel*, a mixed drink long known in Bordeaux which was introduced into the United States by French officers allied to George Washington's army. These famed Gallic volunteers, under the great Lafayette, come into another legend.

It is said that one Betsy Flanagan, widow of a Revolutionary soldier, in 1779 kept a tavern frequented by the French. Next door was a Loyalist, who kept finer chickens than did Betsy. One night she gave a feast for her overseas friends, using her neighbour's fowls which she presumably thought forfeit to the cause of Independence. On this occasion she preceded the repast with bracers of mixed drinks and decorated the bottles containing them with tail feathers from her enemy's prized cocks. In toasting their hostess, and in a display of their partial knowledge of her language, the soldiers shouted 'Vive le cock-tail'.

Bessie Got Muddled

Another tale. An American tavern-owner of the same period would not allow his daughter, Bessie, to espouse an American officer. One day his champion fighting-cock, Washington, disappeared. The distraught owner offered his daughter in marriage to whoever returned the precious bird which, in the sporting circles of the times, would quite likely have been considered more valuable than any female. Surprise! Surprise! The rejected suitor found Washington, and the owner honoured his promise. At the betrothal party, Bessie got so excited that she outrageously mixed up drinks from her father's copious supplies. But the guests found the mixture splendid and named it 'cocktail'.

The great Harry Craddock of the Savoy, London, published in *The Bartender* in 1936 the following exotic story which he had received from Central America. It is the only 'origin of the species' notion given serious attention in *The International Guide to Drinks* of the United Kingdom Bartenders' Guild.

Down Mexico Way

Long ago, at the port of Campeche on the Gulf of Mexico, English sailors discovered the virtues of a local speciality in mixed drinks whose ingredients were traditionally stirred with a wooden spoon. However, one popular bar-keeper used for this purpose a small natural root known from its shape as *cola de gallo*. When the visitors asked what the odd instrument was, its name was translated as 'cock's tail', and this was transferred to the drink itself.

A peculiarly exotic cock*tale* is said – not too seriously – in the *Savoy Cocktail Book* (1965) to be the 'only authentic and incontrovertible story of the origin of the Cocktail ...' It is charming, but in my opinion, absurd. Oscar C. Mendelsohn in his invaluable *The Dictionary of Drinks and Drinking* calls it 'one of the crazier theories'. Briefly, here it is.

Xoctl, lovely daughter of a Mexican king, served a strong, strange and palatable mixture to visiting American officers. The meeting was satisfactory, and the American general in charge said he would see to it their charming hostess was immortalized in the Army. The nearest anyone could get to pronouncing the charmer's name was 'Cocktail' – and there you are!

Ole Man Cocktail

A final story, which I have seen but once in print – and that in a private publication of seventy years ago – places the origin of Cocktail in old-time Mississippi river steamers. It appears that, to relieve the tedium, some successful gambler or rich voyager would call for drinks from every bottle in the bar to be mixed in a large container. A somewhat hectic party would ensue, all passengers partaking freely while supplies lasted. The glasses used for imbibing this sinister concoction had a crude resemblance to the breast of a cock whilst the stirrers customarily provided were similar to that bird's curving tail feathers. Thus, such conglomerations of potables became 'Cocktails'. The illustration to an 1871 ballad, 'An American Cock-Tale' lends some validity to this derivation.

Those are all the legends (?) which *I* have come across. Certainly, a century ago the word Cocktail was well-known as a description for certain mixed drinks, though its use was much more limited than today: Collins, Daisy, Cobbler, Shrub, Fix, Crusta, Rickey, Smash, and other words, were used for compounds which, except in precise expert and professional circles, we would simply call Cocktails.

Trade-produced pre-mixed Cocktails were popular in the United States well before the turn of the century, and later enjoyed a transient vogue in Britain. They are still produced, but their popularity remains *much* higher in the USA than in the UK, though, in the latter, certain fairly inexpensive proprietary non-spirit based 'cocktails' are in steady demand.

The Cocktail Age

The Cocktail Age, which may be said to have lasted from 1920–37, produced a galaxy of Cocktails: there are at least 7,000 recipes. Of these a great majority were ridiculous, and others mere adulterations of classic formulae. The Bright Young Things – and the not quite so bright older ones – made a fetish of odd mixtures and vied in their preparation and consumption. Cocktails were 'fashionable' in the extreme sense of the phrase. The fashion certainly came from America, then in the throes of Prohibition, and it is thought that the need to hide the flavour of 'bath-tub' gin gave great impetus to the invention of new Cocktails, and this habit spread, firstly to people with access to good liquor and thence overseas, where those with the means to gratify their crazes found American social habits *chic*. For only a fringe of urban populations then really took up the Cocktail, though these were the people of influence. Repeal of Prohibition in the States made legal, and accentuated, a custom already well-established.

In 1930, the first *Savoy Cocktail Book* was published, perhaps the specialized classic in its field. (It has recently been revised and re-published.) The same era also saw the Booth's *Anthology of Cocktails* which is now a collector's item. It reflects the tastes and the snobbery of its age. Celebrities (Lady Oxford, Tom Walls, Ivor Novello, Sybil Thorndike, Beverley Nichols, and many others) had their names linked with Cocktails specially invented for them. Let me quote that for the Earl of Northesk, famous bobsleigh champion. It was called Snowball and consisted of '1/3 Booth's Gin; 1/6 crème de Violette; 1/6 white crème de Menthe; 1/6 anisette, and 1/6 sweet cream'. Typical – but not a modern connoisseur's idea of a Cocktail.

A publication of this period of considerable technical merit, to which I have found no reference in modern bibulous commentaries, is *The Barkeeper's Golden Book*, sub-titled *The Exquisite Book of American Drinks*, by O. Blunier, who describes himself proudly as 'Barkeeper'. Published in a trilingual (English, French, German) edition in 1935, this volume divides mixed drinks into twenty-four distinct categories on Johnson lines, but with a number of omissions (Crusta, Shrub, Smash) and several additions, including High Ball (*sic*).

M. Blunier, who ran a successful speak-easy in New York during Prohibition – his illustration of it gives it the appearance of a smart legitimate Bar – lists 16 as the minimum drinks for a private Bar and 124 as the optimum for a fully-stocked hotel Bar. Essentially a detailed volume for the professional or expert and well-heeled amateur, *The Barkeeper's Golden Book* does contain recipes still valid while emphasizing how right we are nowadays to simplify our codings and limit our recipes numerically. The introduction contains the rather charming statement: 'Certainly, a bartender who serves "the

27

world and his wife" in a faithful and modest manner, acquires a lofty and well-balanced conception of life.'

Towards the end of the thirties the Cocktail Age had run its course, its image considerably brought into disrepute by the excesses of some of those foolish young folk with whom it was popularly connected. The more sedate, cheaper – and duller – Sherry party replaced the Cocktail Party in many circles. Gin-and-tonic was gaining a hold it never was to lose. Clouds loomed on the horizon which made distasteful to thinking people the seemingly perpetual celebrations of the Cocktail Age. It was a time to be serious. Then came war – and the cocktail-drinkers became officers and administrators; and a most successful metamorphosis they performed.

Changing Patterns

The end of World War II found the social patterns of many countries changed. In the USA – and in Europe after an austerity-ridden period of re-settlement – wealth was more evenly distributed. Habits of good living were not the per-quisite of a few leaders of Fashion and their followers. Thus we come to our own present time and its drinking patterns, in the context of this chapter.

That Cocktails are widely – but no longer wildly – enjoyed is witnessed by a number of successful publications concerned with them. While the more expensive and comprehensive of these volumes still tend to involve themselves in an excessive number of recipes, the best reflect both a wider desire for knowledge on the subject and a more educated approach by a comparatively affluent populace. The 'classic' recipes have weathered the passage of time – the Dry Martini (see Chapter 3), the Bronx, the Manhattan, and a handful of others.

The New York Bartenders' Union says that perhaps as many as fifty Cocktails are regularly served in the United

States. Mr Oscar Mendelsohn suggests that less than half that number have real popularity in the British Commonwealth, and I think he is right. However, it must be conceded that a large number of people like to read about Cocktails they may never actually make, just as they will absorbedly peruse recipes in *haute cuisine* they will never cook, or will study books on vintage wines they will never have the fortune to taste.

In my own experience with correspondents, I have noted over the last three years a growing interest in Cocktails – or perhaps I should say in Mixed Drinks – for home entertainment. In part, this may be attributed to the emergence of Home Bars as a status symbol; bar equipment is well displayed in department stores, so it is obviously in demand by the public.

Cocktail Parties are regularly reported as being given by the highest social arbiters. An increasing sophistication of mass taste, a growing awareness of the merits, and sheer fun, of certain habits previously condemned as belonging to a different 'class', will not bring (thank God) another Cocktail Age. But they will enlarge a sensible appreciation of, in the broadest sense, that thing of strange origin – the Cocktail.

'The great majority of the English move inside much too narrow an ambit of drinks, and many lives move between tea and beer.'

Douglas Woodruff

CHAPTER 3

The Dry Martini Mystique

NO COCKTAIL – nor any mixed drink – has more *mystique*,
folklore, legend and anecdote surounding it than the Dry
Martini. It is an absolute fetish in widespread social circles in
America, its devotees are international, and the Dry Martini
cult is highly developed in Britain, where I believe the greatest expert to be my own boss. (Though I cannot match
his extraordinary palate for detecting the minutest alteration
in the ingredients, I share his delight in this supreme concoction – while disagreeing with him on certain details
of preparation.)

Methods of mixing alone will be happily discussed by Dry
Martinians for the entire duration of a party, and, while I may
be prejudiced, I honestly think this chapter will be of some
amusement to those (poor souls!) who do not relish the
Cocktail itself. This cannot pretend to approach a definitive
work on the subject, and I would be grateful to receive pertinent stories, facts or fables from interested readers.

I accept as the most likely origin of the Dry Martini that it
all started in the Waldorf-Astoria hotel, New York City, and
with a bartender named Martini (or, some allege, Martinez). I
cannot date the invention but presumably it was pre-1919
when Prohibition scarred the USA. On the other hand, the
said Martini might have come up with his brainwave for use
at private parties during the time when the open sale of
liquor was illegal, and when never did more flow.

Alchemist's Touch

At any rate, it seems that this genius – who recognized that some of the greatest innovations are the simplest – took what had previously been just a gin and French vermouth and, by the alchemy of stirring the mixture in a separate container, transmogrified it into the Dry Martini, thus changing the drinking habits of the sophisticated world.

Because his name was what it was, he used Martini dry vermouth, well-known in the USA but which essentially implied sweet red Italian vermouth in Britain at that time. Eventually the Dry Martini was to make Martini & Rossi internationally as famous for their very dry pale vermouth as for their other products. In Britain, Dry Martinians will discuss the rival merits of Martini dry and Noilly Prat.

Writing in *The Queen*, Mr Cyril Ray says that at the Martini Terrace in London he was given a Dry Martini by the official bartender which consisted of 2 measures of dry gin to one of vermouth. However, in their own publication the Martini people themselves list a Dry Martini as consisting of – and I quote them –

'$\frac{3}{4}$ Booth's "High & Dry" Gin;
'$\frac{1}{4}$ Martini Dry Vermouth;
'Mixing-glass with ice;
'Squeeze of lemon peel in the cocktail-glass.'

That is an excellent drink, but with all respect to my good friends at Martini & Rossi, it simply is *not* a Dry Martini as it is understood by *cognoscenti* today. The ingredients are fine: it is the proportions with which I disagree.

More Than A Bow

Now, I don't go along with the bartender who allegedly only

let the shadow of the vermouth bottle fall across the gin, nor with his colleague who merely stirred the gin and ice and bowed in the direction of France! I say it should be approximately (one can't actually measure it) one-twelfth vermouth to eleven-twelfths gin; certainly never weaker than a 1:7 ratio. I also opine that to use less than 2 fluid ounces of gin per Cocktail is not worth the effort of stirring.

There are some who believe vermouth is unnecessary, and there is a 'Non-Conformist' school in the USA which drinks 'House of Lords' gin on the rocks in a special brandy-style goblet: that is a 'Snifterini' – splendid, but *not* a Dry Martini. Mr David A. Embury says a real Dry Martini made with this gin, his favourite, is sometimes called a Golden Martini.

I maintain (this is necessarily a rather heavily personalized chapter, and I anticipate some lively *ripostes*) that a Dry Martini must contain the finest London dry gin and top quality dry vermouth. No other ingredients. A similar drink made with vodka is a Vodkatini; this has a certain vogue, but it is *not* a Dry Martini. Nor is the substitution of dry sherry for vermouth acceptable to purists.

However, my pal Eddie Clark, former famous bartender, owner of London's Albemarle Club and author of several cocktail books (*Shaking in the Sixties*, etc.) insists that a Dry Martini contain a dash of orange bitters. So does André Simon. I consider this usage archaic. It is not unknown for a dash of Pernod to be added, but such adulteration is deplorably smarty-smarty.

As for preparation. I go for a large mixing jug (I own a beautiful 3-pint one) and a great deal of ice, clean and in big lumps. Ingredients in; quick stir; strain almost at once. So I was interested when I sat next to an American one day at lunch and we fell to talking about – you've guessed! He was very much against my practice. No, a Dry Martini should be stirred briskly exactly two hundred times, making sure it is one hundred times in one direction and one hundred in the other. A fervent Martinian friend pleads with me to stir thoroughly, but to take out the ice *before* pouring: that is when, says he, too much dilution occurs.

Mr Bernard De Voto was bang on the mark when he stated (*Harper's Magazine*, Dec. 1949): 'Sound practice begins with ice.' He quoted a friend who ended his recipe for the perfect Dry Martini '... and five hundred pounds of ice.' Mr De Voto, who damned the Manhattan Cocktail as 'an offence against piety', highly praised the Dry Martini, insisting on the need for speed and condemning the economical habit of retaining any of the Cocktail in the pitcher where it will become weak: never make more than is required for a single round. Nor should such extravagances as silver cups be used; a stemmed glass is the proper container. However, Mr De Voto's recommended 3·7 : 1 gin/vermouth ratio (got your scales and mathematical tables with you?) does not conform to contemporary taste.

Knock-out Drops

Instead of using ice, one not very powerful branch of the Dry Martini empire employs metal or plastic objects of which the liquid content is frozen; thus the Cocktail is chilled without dilution. Yet it may be argued that a *slight* measure of dilution is not only beneficial but is an essential aspect of a Dry Martini. Not so, say others, filling a jug with gin and a splash of vermouth and incarcerating the whole for total refrigeration, thus producing a drink whose frigidity is only matched by its lethal qualities. I think that method, alcoholically effective as it is, takes the fun out of mixing a Dry Martini – the merry tinkle of the ice, the expertise needed to judge the precise quantities.

I don't know if he was the first, but James Bond Esquire caused some consternation in part of the world of the Dry Martini when he asked for a 'Dry Martini – shaken, not stirred'. It has long been the united opinion of all but a fringe group that a Dry Martini must be stirred, it being held that brusque shaking 'bruises the gin'. I can't believe subtle, but essentially robust, gin bruises easily despite the knocks it has received historically (see Chapter 4) – but this is a pretty conceit I am sorry to see attacked. Aesthetically, and by tradition, a Dry Martini should be stirred, and in glass. Mr Embury asserts that a shaken Dry Martini becomes a Bradford: I wish he said *why*.

It is open to doubt whether a 'Dry Martini on the rocks' – gin and a touch of dry vermouth in a tumbler filled with ice cubes – is a Dry Martini at all. For it hasn't been *made*. Yet it has a certain merit; dilution is speedy in a crowded room and convivial intoxication minimized.

On the other hand, pre-mix bottled Dry Martinis must qualify as the real thing; though I cannot see them pleasing the expert, who will have his own formula, his preferred gin, his particular vermouth. To me they smack of laziness, and lack of both knowledge and initiative: the ready-made bow-tie of the Dry Martini world – there's a danger of becoming unbuttoned!

'*Got an olive?*'

Rex North once told in the *Daily Mirror* the story of the American visitor to the Red Lion Distillery in London who was impressed by the great copper stills and then stood silently before the giant blending containers holding tens of thousands of gallons of gin. After a few minutes he turned to his guide and said 'Got an olive?'

Personally, I don't see that putting an olive in a Dry Martini does much for the Cocktail, or the olive; but good olives are a pleasing 'nibble' while imbibing. As for the addition of a pearl onion, this turns a Dry Martini into a Gibson Cocktail.

Most Dry Martinians know of the American (nearly all Dry Martini anecdotes revolve round Americans) who watched a bartender expertly mixing his Cocktail. When the man reached for a slice of lemon rind, the customer stopped him. 'When I want fruit salad, I'll ask for it,' he said.

This is quite a vexed question. *Is* the answer a lemon? I think it must be left to personal taste. I feel that the immersion of lemon rind in the drink imparts too fruity a flavour; but the squeezing of a sliver of rind above the glass, thus releasing a few invisible droplets of citric oil on to it, adds a subtle something. It seems a tendency of bartenders, probably through popular demand, to put the rind into the drink: total immersion is a religious, not a bar, ritual. One should make one's precise requirements known. And speaking of this, at least in Britain, if one wants a really *dry* Dry Martini one should be prepared, and declare one's willingness, to pay for the higher percentage of gin, for the Cocktail is often priced on the basis of around one-quarter to one-sixth vermouth.

Now We are Three

The Dry Martini game is said to be played like this: the story is, of course, American. Four old friends, who are true Dry Martinians, assemble. Beside the tables of each of them is a pitcher containing a pint of Dry Martinis. These Cocktails they ingest within twenty minutes. One of the friends then goes from the room: the game is for the other three to find out who has left!

Dry Martinis, as usually made today, do tend to be rather powerful. And, to repeat one of my own apophthegms: 'There is no such thing as *one* Dry Martini'. It is with candour

35

tinged with regret that I recall that the central character (Ray Milland) of the memorable, horrifying and most thirst-inducing of motion pictures, *The Lost Weekend*, indulged (funds permitting) in Dry Martinis. The Dry Martini is not for the weak-headed or the weak-willed. Over-indulgence will produce self-confidence combined with aggressiveness – one secretary I know has christened this the DMNs (Dry Martini Niggles) and knows how to deal with them – but some people achieve that condition by far less civilized processes!

The real Dry Martinian is never the worse for drink – only the better for it: for his drink is the most civilized, famous, appetizing, interesting, stimulating, cleanest of all Cocktails.

'I must get out of these wet clothes and into a Dry Martini.'
Alexander Woollcott

CHAPTER 4

Gin – The Cinderella Spirit

IF ONLY because gin is the most suitable and widely used spirit for Cocktails and mixed drinks, it must be given pride of place in a tome primarily devoted to those subjects. One might add that no less an authority than André Simon calls it (*A Dictionary of Wines, Spirits and Liqueurs*) '... the purest of all spirits', while L. W. Marrison (Penguin's *Wines and Spirits*) dubs it the world's 'most popular'. David A. Embury (*The Fine Art of Mixing Drinks*) names gin as 'first amongst the liquors used as a Cocktail base ...' It is generally conceded today that gin is a salubrious and versatile spirit, enjoyed all over the civilized world at every level of society. Yet my *Chamber's Encyclopaedia* of 1878 – not so long ago in gin's history – refers to gin scathingly as 'the common drink of the lower classes in London and its vicinity', and makes unflattering comments on some processes of its then manufacture by certain producers. Quite a change in status in under a century.

However, we must go back to the 16th century Netherlands for a start. It would appear that it was the Medical Faculty of the University of Leyden – authorities differ on both the time and man involved – that introduced a spirit distilled from rye and flavoured with juniper. This may have had some connexion with an earlier juniper-flavoured wine known in France as 'the wine of the poor'. This new potion was invented as a medicine, combining the diuretic properties of oil of juniper with the stimulant virtues of alcohol (and the connexion between gin and physical well-being has endured in the opinion of generations).

Long before this, English soldiers had found the primitive 'aquavit' spirits of the Low Countries helpful against the prevailing damp and distinctly encouraging prior to the hazards of battle. To this we owe the expression 'Dutch courage'. In due course, the elixir compounded at Leyden permeated outside medical circles: in 1575 Lucas Bols established a distillery in Amsterdam, and it is deduced that he produced gin of a sort.

Linguistic Problems

The new liquor needed a name. Polite language then being mainly conducted in French, and the French for juniper being *genièvre*, it appears that this word was attached to the spirit. The Dutch equivalent was *jenever* (sometimes spelt *genever*) which the English – with a talent for linguistic corruption; e.g. Leghorn for dulcet Livorno – chose to make *geneva*. This caused a long-term and totally erroneous association of gin with Switzerland, so that gin is still known as *Ginebra* in parts of South America, that being the Spanish for the Swiss city.

Mr L. W. Marrison asserts that gin comes from the Italian *ginevra*, but I don't see where Italy comes into the picture. Presumably, *geneva* was pronounced *gineva* by the English, and the whole thing Anglicized, and shortened to *gin* when the spirit caught on in England. (Though for a time the other terms, plus Hollands, were also used).

Enough of semantics. In future our subject will simply be called gin.

Though he did not at that time have a Field-Marshal's baton in his knapsack, that useful luggage of many a returning English soldier must have held a flagon of the new improved

Dutch elixir. Traders with the Netherlands also played their part in introducing the spirit. The English were traditionally drinkers of beer and wine, and English distilling was in its infancy, but some brewers took to producing the juniper-flavoured spirit – probably pretty crude stuff – and it began to enjoy a certain favour, notably in ports.

Until Charles I granted a charter to the Worshipful Company of Distillers, distilling in England was uncontrolled. Both Charles II and James II granted brewers distillation rights to encourage the use of home-grown grains. But during these reigns the importation of French brandy was encouraged, so gin did not make great headway.

When James II fled, and to France at that, importation of brandy ceased – at least legally. It became patriotic to drink English-distilled spirit; that is, gin. In the next year William III, with his co-Sovereign Mary, ascended the throne. Coming from the original home of gin, he would hardly discourage its consumption. In 1690, gin consumption was 500,000 gallons. By 1729 it was nearly 5,000,000 gallons.

One in Four

In the Cities of London and Westminster, it was thought that one in four houses sold gin, doubtless much of it deplorable since Queen Anne revoked the charter of the Distillers livery company who alone could exercise effective controls.

There were well over 7,000 regular dram-shops in the metropolitan area, of which we may perhaps remember only the one in Southwark, which carried the infamous and much-quoted legend 'Drunk for 1*d*.; dead drunk for 2*d*.; clean straw for nothing'. Gin was sold in street markets, hawked from door to door, and sometimes given in lieu of wages.

Insobriety was a national vice; but I will repeat here what I have elsewhere put forward as a thinking point. During the considerable period when a large number of the labouring masses were apparently in a state of permanent intoxication, and their rulers steadily inebriated on costlier potables, these two social extremes – aided by a by no means abstemious commercial class, and with a hard-drinking literary and artistic coterie to record their prowess – were building up the greatest Empire known to man. It does not seem that sobriety and national greatness are necessarily synonymous.

In the 18th century life was rough and short for almost everyone, and certainly undiluted metropolitan water, as a thirst-quencher, tendered partially comprehended perils. Alcohol was usually the sole refuge from the sheer sordidness of life endured by the urban proletariat. While excesses there were indeed, gin also was *popular*: therefore – such being a fixation with legislators ancient and modern – there must be something rather wrong about it! So reform was demanded, and Westminster went ham-handedly into action. In 1729 a tax was imposed on gin and a licence enforced for retailers. However, in drafting the Act only gin was specified, and this left outside the law crude, unflavoured spirit: Cockney wit christened it 'Parliamentary Brandy'.

This futile Act was repealed and replaced by another which effectively prevented the sale of gin other than from dwelling houses: this turned many an additional house into a booze-den. In 1736, Parliament introduced a new Gin Act, which would, had it been possible to enforce it, virtually have entailed Prohibition – at least for those who could not afford costlier wines and spirits. The Act forbade the retailing of spirits in less quantities than 2 gallons, plus a duty of £1 a gallon and a licence of £50. This led to widespread evasion; the law brought into contempt; murder of informers; riot; loss to the revenue; a disproportionate number of convictions, in which the fines imposed were rarely paid; prisons crowded, and drunkenness unabated. A measure of legislative sense prevailed in 1743, which encouraged reputable London distillers to produce wholesome gin.

Still Serious Problem

Our Cinderella spirit was getting on, but she had far from achieved respectability, and Hogarth's 'Gin Lane' was only too valid a comment. There was plenty of poor cheap 'gin' available. Drunkenness continued, and was to continue, a serious urban problem, almost into our present age.

The turn of the century brought the first rumblings of the Industrial Revolution which was to change Britain for ever. Workers began to flock into once sleepy cities, to inhabit those 'model dwellings' which we know as the back-to-back slum houses. They had a little more money than their fathers, were a little less hungry; but amusements were few. So came the Gin Palace, of which the young Dickens writes with little liking in *Sketches by Boz*. Yet the Gin Palace was a near vital social necessity. It provided warmth, the glamour of brass and mirror and gaslight, sociable company – and, of course, gin. Not only gin, to be sure, but a great deal of gin. What an improvement on the sordid grog-shops of the past. (It is rather amusing that the brewers, after tearing down some remarkable Gin Palaces, are putting up many 'Victorian' replicas.)

The Gin Palace was not popular with the ruling classes. George Cruikshank, Dicken's illustrator, who in his youth liked a convivial noggin, savagely attacked gin and its palaces. How was he to realize that in a century's time gin would be as acceptable in real palaces as it was with the plebs of his own time?

A Temperance Movement was growing apace, though most of those who condemned drinking by the workers were, by the sober standards of today, tippling considerably in their own domiciles; nor was it unknown for their womenfolk privately to take a drop of gin on the grounds of health. Parliament once more decided to legislate, there being no one around to remind them of the folly of the previous century's Gin Acts. In 1871 an Act was introduced which went a long way to trying to impose Prohibition: it would have halved the number of public houses in England and Wales. Mass opinion was incensed. The toilers did not lack their protectors, however. Opposing the Bill in the House of Lords, one Bishop opined he would prefer to see 'England free better than England sober'. The Bill was withdrawn, and when he was defeated at the polls three years later, Mr Gladstone commented that he had been 'borne down in a torrent of gin . . .'

Respectability Achieved

Even earlier than this (see Chapter 2), Cocktails made with gin were being drunk, at least in the United States, and probably in England. In the 1880s, an American opened a saloon in the vicinity of the Bank of England, purveying mixed drinks, mainly based on gin. While it was to be thirty years before London's first American Bar opened, gin drinks were certainly known and reasonably respectable long before then. Gin, with fruit juices, or quinine water (Tonic) had caught on with Britain's far-flung imperial administrators who brought the habit back with them. Gin with bitters (and the Royal Navy officers' 'pink gin') was quite commonplace, and at the beginning of this century gin, with vermouth or other additives, was acceptable in sections of Society.

The famous Harry's New York Bar ('sank roo doe noo') opened in Paris in 1911, and claims to have added the Sidecar and White Lady Cocktails to the world's repertoire. At

Harry's in 1924 was founded the International Bar Flies club.

The acceptance of gin as a universal, and not just a 'lower class', spirit is impossible to date with any precision: it was a gradual process. I think we may place its earliest beginnings with the introduction of unsweetened gin, which began to be popular in the seventies, though it appears to have been in commerce twenty years before then. To confuse the issue, there is a reference to *un*sweetened 'Old Tom' gin in a lawsuit of 1903 (see note 2 of the addendum to this Chapter), but it is possible this is a misprint in the records. On the other hand, while we think of 'Old Tom' as a sweet gin, this may not have been the case when very sugary 'cordial' gins were much used.

'Old Tom' is rarely seen in Britain nowadays, though it is exported from London to Finland and a few other markets, and enjoys a certain vogue in the USA, notably in California where the 'Cat and Barrel' brand has a following.

Elegant glass, and china, urns – still occasionally to be found in pubs and of which fine examples are collector's pieces – bearing the words 'Unsweetened Gin', and usually with a proprietary name, became frequent by 1890. Soon distillers were speaking of their 'dry' gin, stating that it contained no added sugar.

So we arrive at 'London Dry Gin'. This is the type of gin in general commerce throughout the world. It is generally accepted that the absolute best of all London dry gin is distilled only in London itself. The premier brands produced overseas carry the truly famous old London names and quality control is exercised in London. There are a few non-London firms making good dry gins, but there are some terrible foreign ones that are sometimes labelled to suggest, at a cursory glance, that they are, say, by Booth's or Gordon's.

It Didn't Stand a Chance

After World War I, the United States decided to embark on an experiment in Prohibition, in spite of all historic evidence from other countries that, either totally or partially, such an endeavour must fail. However, despite the opprobrium attaching to the widely-used 'bath-tub' gin, gin as such gained tremendous impetus and enhanced social acceptance. Bootlegged gin poured into the States, and real London dry gin was first tasted by many Americans during Prohibition.

In 1933, a further constitutional amendment returned to individual States the control of liquor laws. At least two important English distillers then commenced production in the US, and (legal) export from London started again. By this time, gin was universally established in every respect: our Cinderella had finally arrived.

London dry gin, as distilled by the principal London distillers, starts as a pure spirit. It is then rectified (redistilled) and at the same time flavoured with the essential juniper (which is held by many to make gin the healthiest of spirits), coriander, and a much smaller number of botanical ingredients whose variety and percentage vary with the closely guarded formulae of the brand owners.

Theoretically, it is extremely simple to make gin. That only a *very* few firms distil absolutely top grade gin proves the great difference between theory and practice!

NOTES ON GIN

1. Dutch Gin or Hollands. This is now so different from London dry gin that it must be treated as an entirely different spirit. Bols and De Kuyper are the best known brands in Britain. An excellent drink at its best, for the Dutch are fine distillers, it is rather highly flavoured and is really not suitable for mixed drinks. Being a form of Schnapps, it is best drunk ice cold in small tots, and may with advantage be washed down with a good Dutch lager.

2. **'Old Tom' Gin.** *The Life and Uncommon Adventures of Captain Dudley Bradstreet* (1775) tells how this gamekeeper turned poacher – he was formerly a government nark – evaded the Act of 1736. 'Having got an acquaintance to take a house in Blue Anchor Alley . . . I purchased in Moorfields the Sign of a Cat and had it nailed to a street window. I then caused a lead pipe, the small end out about an inch, to be placed under the paw of the Cat: the end that was in had a funnel to it. I got up early next morning . . . at last I heard the chink of money and a comfortable voice say: "Puss, give me two pennyworth of gin." I immediately put my mouth to the tube and bid them receive it from the pipe . . .' Bradstreet made a lot of money, constantly changing the address of his business. The present site of the Cat would soon be passed around the parish, and possibly this feline association with gin gave rise to 'Old Tom' as one descriptive synonym. Anyway, Bradstreet's mobile 'speak-easy' must rank as a pioneer 'coin-op' enterprise!

From the lawsuit of *Boord and Son* v. *Huddart* (1903), we learn that, about 1849, Boord's of London (founded in 1726 and still a brand name famous in some countries though no longer owning a distillery) adopted a Tom-cat on a barrel – their trademark – with the title 'Old Tom'. Tradition had it that a cat once fell into a vat and the gin therefrom was thought much improved! But Boord's established (*Encyclopaedia Britannica* 11th edition) that the term 'Old Tom' was much older and came from an actual person, Thomas Chamberlain of Hodge's Distillery, an experimenter with gin flavouring, and one of the ancient Boord's labels showed a picture of 'Old Tom' Chamberlain.

N.B.: A Tom Collins Cocktail is made with Old Tom Gin. A John Collins is made with Dry Gin.

3. Historic Names for Gin. Gin has in the past had a great many popular names – rude, affectionate or secretive. This list is not definitive, far from it:

Some, from *The Book of the Wine-Label* by N. M. Penzer – (names used to evade the Act of 1736) Cream of the Valley; Sangree; Tom Roe; Cuckold's Comfort; Make Shift; Last Shift; Ladies' Delight; The Baulk; Gripe Water; King Theodore of Corsica. 'White Wine' was used as a euphemism for gin in polite Victorian society, and the same affectation was sometimes practised by having a label inscribed 'Nig' round the gin decanter neck.

Apparently this was also intended to deceive servants – which I am sure it wouldn't have done for a day! Some authorities give 'Nig' as back slang, but its genteel usage seems confirmed by actual decanter labels that have survived.

Best known of slang names for gin is certainly Mother's Ruin. There are also Lap (chorus girls' slang); Daffy's elixir (from an 18th century patent medicine); Snaps (corruption of Schnapps); Eye-water (said to be printers' slang in *The True Drunkard's Delight*); Bryan O'Lynn (rhyming slang); Blue Ruin; Cat's Water; Flash of Lightning ... I think that will do.

4. Plymouth Gin. A distinct type of gin, rather more aromatic than London Dry, but considerably less so than

Hollands. The traditional base for pink gin (q.v.), though many people take this drink with London dry gin. Closely associated with the city of Plymouth and the firm of Coates and Co.

5. Other Gins. Orange gin, Lemon gin (I have seen Apple gin) can be bought but have much shrunk in popularity since the war. They may be made at home quite simply. Sloe gin is probably the most popular of these 'gins', though correctly it should be classified as a cordial: it also is widely made at home when the sloe crop is good. But you have to buy the gin first! (Gin recipe 40.) A low-strength blackcurrant gin is now being imported from the Continent.

6. Gin and Health. We know gin was invented for medicinal reasons. To quote the *New Era Illustrated* of December, 1934: 'Gin is recommended by many important physicians. It has very beneficial effects in disorders such as gout, rheumatism and any form of bladder or kidney complaints, and women have for many years appreciated the necessity of taking gin as a remedy for the minor ailments to which their sex is subject.' That is a pretty strong statement on which it would be unwise for me to comment, except to say that I have *personally* found that 'Booth's' gin, taken only with Malvern Water, is beneficial for *my* gout. I'm not saying it will do the same for everyone. Also I find, party-wise, that exclusive devotion to the same drink is non-productive of matutinal malaise.

As an historical sidelight one may aptly recall the little-known effect of gin on the Battle of Waterloo. Marshal Blücher was thrown from his horse at a crucial stage in his march to bring the vital reinforcements awaited by the Duke of Wellington. He was revived with a massage of *Gin* and onions. Of course, he might have made it without this aid – but who knows?

'When the clergyman's daughter drinks nothing but water, she's certain to finish on gin.'

Rudyard Kipling

General Note on Recipes

To avoid constant repetition, it should be taken for granted that all drinks should be stirred or shaken with plenty of *ICE*. Where ice is added separately, I have indicated this. The odd occasions where no ice is required are clear enough.

Italicized words below recipes refer to their source – as far as I am concerned – where this may be of interest, or I feel extra acknowledgement is due. (UKBG refers to the authoritative guide to drinks of the United Kingdom Bartenders' Guild, the influential body to which belong a majority of British professional Bartenders).

Where ingredients are not represented by proportions of ingredients to the total drink, in fractions, the fluid ounce – simply 'oz.' – is used as the basic measure (see Chapter 18).

Books of reference differ considerably in regard to long-established mixed drinks: I have chosen the recipe I think best or my personal edition of it. (Certain explanatory notes are appended where of instructive or general interest). Names of mixed drinks have over the years got very mixed themselves: where a drink has become particularly popular in association with one base, it tends to be adopted by quite a different one. Thus, I have seen a Bronx listed as made with whiskey, though it is a famous gin Cocktail.

With many drinks it is essential to test them – this is particularly true of Punches – during making. Degrees of sweetness, if only that, are very much a personal matter.

References to 'powdered sugar' mean fine (but not icing) sugar. A good alternative idea is to prepare a bottle of sugar syrup by boiling 1 lb. sugar in 1 pint water. This may be stored in a refrigerator and used as required. Similar quantities of dry or wet sweetening apply.

> 'Learn all the rules, every one of them, so that you will know how to break them.'
>
> *I. S. Cobb*

GIN COCKTAILS AND SUNDRY MIXED DRINKS

1. Alaska

¾ Dry Gin
¼ Yellow Chatreuse

Shake, strain into cocktail-glass.

2. Antonio

⅓ Dry Gin
⅓ Brandy
⅙ Maraschino Drioli
⅙ Crème de Menthe

Shake well and strain into cocktail-glass.

3. Baccio Punch

1 bottle Dry Gin
1 bottle pure Grapefruit Juice
1 bottle Champagne
Siphon Soda-Water
½ bottle Anisette

Mix in large bowl (other than the Champagne) with large lumps of ice. Add fruit in season and, at last moment, chilled Champagne.

4. Betty James

½ Dry Gin
¼ Lemon Juice
¼ Maraschino
1 dash Angostura

Shake, and strain into cocktail-glass.

5. Booth's Party Punch

for about 12 persons:
6 wine-glasses 'Booth's' Gin
1 wine-glass Cointreau
½ wine-glass Brandy
Juice of 3 Lemons
Heaped tablespoon Powdered Sugar

Mix well in glass bowl or jug, add flagon fizzy Lemonade and plenty of ice. Decorate with round of Cucumber.

Serve in wine-glasses.

6. Bronx

½ Dry Gin
¼ Sweet Vermouth
¼ Dry Vermouth
Juice of ¼ Orange

Shake, strain into cocktail-glass.

7. Clover Club

⅔ Dry Gin
⅓ Grenadine
Juice of ½ Lemon
White of 1 Egg

Shake very briskly; strain into wine-glass.

8. Dry Martini

It would be ridiculous to try to give a recipe here after what has been written in Chapter 3.

9. Fibber McGee

1½ oz. Dry Gin
½ oz. Unsweetened Grapefruit Juice
½ oz. Sweet Vermouth
2 dashes Angostura

Stir, strain into cocktail-glass; add twist Lemon rind.

10. Flying High

(Evolved by the author for an airline occasion)
1½ oz. 'High & Dry' Gin

1 oz. fresh Orange Juice
1 oz. Cherry Heering Cherry Brandy
Teaspoon Lemon Juice
Dash of Angostura
White of an Egg

Shake very briskly and strain into wine-glass.

11. Fun and Games

½ 'Booth's' Gin
¼ Blackcurrant Cordial (Cassis)
¼ fresh Lemon Juice
Dash Angostura

Shake well and strain into cocktail-glass.
Serve with small segment of Lemon.
J. D./Booth's

12. Gibson

A Dry Martini served with a Cocktail Onion.

13. Gimlet

½ Dry Gin
½ Rose's Lime Juice Cordial

Shake and strain into cocktail-glass.
Mr Raymond Chandler's edition

14. Gin Cocktail

2 oz. Dry Gin
5 dashes Orange Bitters

Shake, strain into cocktail-glass.

15. Gin Fizz

1 oz. Dry Gin
Juice of ½ large Lemon
½ tablespoon Powdered Sugar

Shake well; strain into wine-glass; top with Soda-Water.

16. Gin-Gin

Equal measures 'Booth's' Gin; Crabbie's Green Ginger Wine; Orange Squash

Shake vigorously and strain into large cocktail-glass.
Booth's

17. Gin-and-It (or French)

Simply Dry Gin with 'Italian' (sweet) or 'French' (dry) Vermouth, poured directly into the glass in proportions to individual taste, possibly with ice and a twist of Lemon rind.

18. Gin Rickey

Over ice in tumbler pour 2 oz. Dry Gin; 1 oz. fresh Lime or Lemon Juice; dash of Grenadine Syrup; twist of rind. Top with Soda-Water.

Note: a Rickey may be made with any spirit.

19. Gin Sling

Juice of small Lemon
Heaped teaspoon Powdered Sugar
1½ oz. Dry Gin
Dash of Angostura

Mix in tumbler with ice cubes, top with water.

20. Gin Sour

2 oz. Dry Gin
½ oz. Lemon Juice
Teaspoon Sugar Syrup
Dash of Orange Bitters

Shake, strain into large cocktail-glass.

This may also be made with other spirits – Whisky Sour, Brandy Sour, etc. – and may also be served as a long drink. Proportions are a matter for individual taste.

21. Gin Swizzle

1½ oz. Dry Gin
¾ oz. Unsweetened Lime Juice
Teaspoon Sugar Syrup
2 dashes Angostura

Mix vigorously until very cold; strain into large cocktail-glass.

(Swizzles may be made with any preferred spirit but Gin is perhaps the most satisfactory).

22. Gloom Chaser

1½ oz. Dry Gin
1 oz. Dry Vermouth
½ teaspoon Grenadine
2 dashes Pernod.
Shake, strain into cocktail-glass.

23. Golden Martini

A Dry Martini Cocktail made to personal preference, using 'Booth's' Gin.

24. Golf

1 oz. Dry Gin
½ oz. Dry Vermouth
2 dashes Angostura

Stir, strain into cocktail-glass. Serve with Olive.
Trader Vic

25. Gordon's Cup

Using large glass with ice; ½ glass 'Gordon's' Gin; ½ glass
Port; fill with Tonic-Water or Lemonade; garnish with 1
slice Cucumber; 1 slice Lemon; crushed Mint Leaves.
Tanqueray Gordon and Co.

26. Horse's Neck

Hang continuous spiral of Lemon Peel in tall glass. Add
ice cubes; at least 2 oz. Dry Gin. Top with Canada Dry
Ginger Ale.

Note: may also be made with Whisky, Brandy or light Rum.

27. Ideal

1 oz. Dry Gin
½ oz. Dry Vermouth
½ oz. fresh Grapefruit Juice
Teaspoon Powdered Sugar
2 dashes Angostura

Shake, strain into cocktail-glass; garnish with Cocktail
Cherry.

28. John Collins

1 oz. Dry Gin
½ tablespoon Powdered Sugar
Juice of ½ Lemon

Pour over ice cubes in tumbler. Top with Soda-Water; stir.

29. Lichee

Equal parts—
Dry Gin
Dry Vermouth
Lichee Syrup (from can of fruit)
3 dashes Angostura

Shake, strain into cocktail-glass. Serve with canned Lichee on stick.

30. Londoner

1½ oz. 'High & Dry' Gin
½ oz. Rose Hip Syrup
Juice of ½ Lemon
½ oz. Martini Dry Vermouth

Pour over ice in tall glass; stir thoroughly and top with Soda-Water; add round of Lemon.
Booth's

31. My Fair Lady

1 oz. Gin
½ oz. Orange Juice
½ oz. Lemon Juice

1 teaspoon Fraise Liqueur
White of one Egg

Shake well, strain into cocktail-glass.
Savoy

32. Negroni

2 oz. Dry Gin
1 oz. Sweet Vermouth
1 oz. Campari

Pour over ice in tall goblet; top with Soda-Water; add slice of Orange.

33. Old Etonian

½ Gin
½ Lillet
2 dashes Orange Bitters
2 dashes Crème de Noyau

Shake, strain into cocktail-glass. Squeeze Orange peel on top.

34. Orange Blossom

½ Dry Gin
½ Orange Juice

Shake, strain into cocktail-glass.

35. Pink Gin

Shake several drops of Angostura Bitters into a wine-glass

or similar sized one. Roll the bitters round the glass and shake out any surplus. Pour in 1½ oz. Gin, with ice, water or Soda-Water according to individual taste.

Usually made with Plymouth Gin, though some people specify other Gins. A gimmick is to set fire to the Angostura in the glass; this merely destroys the drink as far as Pink Gin is understood by its many devotees.

36. Red Lion

1 oz. 'High & Dry' Gin
½ oz. Grand Marnier
¼ oz. Orange Juice
¼ oz. Lemon Juice

Shake, strain into cocktail-glass of which rim is frosted with Powdered Sugar.
  Mr Eddie Clarke

37. Sheep Dip

2 oz. 'High & Dry' Gin
1 oz. Tio Pepe Sherry
1 wine-glass of Medium-Sweet Merrydown Cider

Shake, and strain into large goblet.
  Mr J. Beswick

38. Silver Streak

½ Gin
¼ Lemon Juice
¼ Kummel

Shake, strain into cocktail-glass.

39. Singapore Gin Sling

2 oz. Dry Gin
Juice of a Lemon
Heaped teaspoon Powdered Sugar

Pour over ice in large tall glass; add Soda-Water; ½ oz. Cointreau; ½ oz. Cherry Brandy. Stir. Decorate with slice of Lemon. Serve with straws.

40. Sloe Gin

To make your own (ref. Chapter 4, note 5).
Half fill bottle with fresh Sloes that have been pricked. Add 2 inches of Granulated Sugar. Top up with fine Dry Gin (as dry as possible). Leave for minimum 3 months, shaking once a week. Strain into fresh bottle (adjusting sweetness to individual taste at this stage).

41. South of the Border

1½ oz. 'Booth's' Gin
1 oz. fresh Lemon Juice
1 oz. Kahlua
White of 1 Egg

Shake vigorously and pour whilst still agitating shaker. Decorate with cocktail Cherry.
Booth's

42. Stainless Dry

⅔ 'High & Dry' Gin
⅓ fresh Jaffa Grapefruit Juice. Pour over ice into tall glass. Add teaspoon Cointreau, dash of Angostura Bitters. Top with sparkling Lemonade.
J.D.

43. Tom Collins

See John Collins. But is made with 'Old Tom' style Gin.

44. White Lady

$\frac{1}{2}$ Dry Gin
$\frac{1}{4}$ Lemon Juice
$\frac{1}{4}$ Cointreau
Teaspoon egg white

Shake, strain into cocktail-glass.

CHAPTER 5

Scotch Whisky – A Gift to the World

IT MAY cause distress to some that whisky should have any place in a book about mixed drinks, since many devotees of Scotch hold that this nectar may only be taken neat or with a small dilution of pure water. But the fact is that a great many regular drinkers of Scotch take it with other dilutionary agents (I have met Scotch-and-Tonic fiends) and a number of persons of good taste enjoy Cocktails, Punches and Toddies of whisky. It would indeed be imbibitionary sacrilege, and financial foolery, to abuse a fine old Single Malt or a rare aged blend with unruly additives, but numerous recipes are popular which are based on good Scotch Whisky. While it is not my intention to deal *technically* with individual spirits and other potables, a short informative background may be of interest.

One must not tread lightly on national pride, yet all authorities are confident that whisky was being made in Ireland before it was in Scotland, and until comparatively recent times Scotch was essentially the drink of the Scots, little used elsewhere.

Scotch is unique amongst the many whiskies of the world, and efforts to imitate it have completely failed. A Japanese 'whisky' was marketed for which it was claimed that it was 'pressed from the finest Scottish grapes'! Unfortunately I have lost my bottle of 'whisky', bought in the Piraeus, inscribed, as I remember, 'Doulton's Scotch Whiskey. Produce of Scotland, Athens, Greece'. The Royal Arms surmounted this label, with 'Highest Quality' replacing the familiar '*Dieu et mon droit*', and a 'warrant' read 'By Appointment to His Majesty The Prince of Wales'. Just to add injury to insult, the bottle had formerly contained Messrs Ballantine's excellent distillation!

By laws, almost universally enforced, 'Scotch' may only be applied to whisky wholly produced in Scotland.

Unique and Mysterious

Why Scotch has its peculiar properties is not fully known in any scientific sense; water, peat, grains, and even air, play their part in producing the unique and mysterious spirit.

Certainly, in the 16th century the Scots were producing an *aquavite* which in Gaelic became *usquebaugh* or *uisge beatha* (water of life), to be anglicized to whisky. Burns, a splendid toper, used the term 'usquebae'. It is said that Bonnie Prince Charlie, forced in exile to drink brandy instead of his native drink, succumbed to that stimulant whereas whisky would have preserved him.

In the early 18th century, the English tried to force taxes on the countless small whisky distilleries, and wholesale evasion took place, including a good deal of boot-legging to the north of England. This went on for a long time, even when, after 1823, legal distilling got under proper way.

When Queen Victoria built Balmoral, the Highlands became fashionable and rich peers and members of the new plutocracy bought Scottish estates or erected mock-baronial castles. Though the rage for protected deer forests brought tragedy to the glens, certainly the 'invaders' discovered Scotch whisky and the habit of drinking Scotch spread southwards to the stately homes of England, and thence to all classes. In our own times it largely superseded Irish whiskey.

The great family names in Scotch – Haig, Dewar, Buchanan,

Walker, Grant, Sanderson, Teacher, Bell, and others – go back many generations in the whisky business, and, despite amalgamations, a majority are run by direct descendants of their founders, who tended to be farmers with a useful sideline in distilling.

D.C.L. Founded

Towards the end of the last century, the business was rationalized by the formation of a federation of leading families, The Distillers Company, today a benevolent giant of British industry. There are several notable independent distilleries, and Scotch whisky's global interests are watched over by the Scotch Whisky Association. It is needless to repeat the triumph of Scotch throughout the world, which increases from year to year. It is loved, and has become a status symbol, everywhere that civilization pertains.

Two Types

There are two basic types of Scotch whisky: Malt, and Grain. The former is produced in pot-stills from malted barley only, and has the greatest character of all Scotch whisky, the best coming from the Highlands. There are about one hundred Malt distilleries in Scotland, operating seasonally.

Grain whisky is produced from a mixture of malted and unmalted cereals, distilled in a Coffey (continuous distillation) still. It must be emphasized that both these are true Scotch whiskies. There are only a dozen grain distilleries.

Single Malts – sole product of an individual distillery – are available and are much appreciated by connoisseurs, yet a number of lifelong whisky-drinkers may never taste them or may not even like them. They are much more redolent of the true peaty whisky flavour than the normal brands of commerce, and cost more not only because they are longer matured – seven to twelve years – but are normally of higher strength.

Nearly all Scotch whisky sold is a blend of Malts and Grains, and thirty or even more whiskies may go into an individual formula. It requires vast experience and enormous skill – human skill that is a gift rather than an education, but which seems inheritable – to keep a blend constant.

No Scotch whisky is sold in Britain until it has rested three years in wood, a legal minimum normally exceeded. If the age of a blend is stated on the label it is that of the youngest whisky in it and not an average age.

Formerly whisky was indiscriminately written with or without an 'e'. Today it is usual to spell the products of Scotland (and Canada) whisky, and other whiskies as whiskey: this is a convention without historical precedent.

There are about one hundred brands of Scotch sold on the British market, though a much greater variety is exported. Not even the Scotch Whisky Association can say precisely how many brand names of Scotch exist – I have heard it put in excess of two thousand – but a number are exclusively sold for blending and others are reserved for local use, private clubs and special markets.

In giving Cocktails and Mixed Drinks that may be made with Scotch, I have eschewed such mutations as 'Whisky Tom Collins' (we'll have a Scotch Dry Martini next!) and list only drinks properly based on Scotch by tradition or sense.

> 'Inspiring bold John Barleycorn,
> What dangers thou canst make us scorn!
> Wi' tippeny we fear nae evil;
> Wi' useuebae, we'll face the devil'
> > *Robert Burns*

SOME UNORTHODOX USES FOR SCOTCH

1. Atholl Brose

1½ oz. Scotch Whisky
1 oz. Clear Honey
1 oz. Pure Cream

Mix well in warm glass. Allow to cool.
Or – omit cream, top with hot milk.

2. Black and White Cooler

Pour over ice in tall glass—
1 oz. 'Black and White' Scotch Whisky
3 dashes Crème de Menthe
Top with Soda-Water

Stir.

3. Blood and Sand

½ oz. each—
Scotch Whisky
Cherry Brandy
Orange Juice
Sweet Vermouth

Shake, strain into large cocktail-glass.

4. Bobby Burns

1½ oz. Scotch Whisky
¾ oz. Sweet Vermouth
Teaspoon Benedictine

> Stir well, strain into cocktail glass.
> Squeeze Lemon rind over but do not immerse.

5. Bunny Hug

Equal parts—
Whisky
Gin
Pernod

> Shake well, strain into cocktail-glass.
> (Less a bunny's hug than a bear's!)

6. Churchill

½ Scotch Whisky
⅙ Lime Juice
⅙ Sweet Vermouth
⅙ Cointreau

> Shake, strain into cocktail-glass.
> *Savoy*

7. Commonwealth

½ 'Vat 69' Scotch Whisky
¼ fresh Lemon Juice
¼ Crabbie's Green Ginger Wine
dash Maraschino

> Shake well with ice and strain into cocktail-glass.
> *J.D.*

8. Haig Special

½ 'Haig' Scotch Whisky
¼ Dry Vermouth
¼ fresh Orange Juice

Shake, and strain. Top with grated Nutmeg.

9. Loch Lomond

1½ oz. Scotch Whisky
1 teaspoon Sugar Syrup
2 dashes Angostura

Shake, strain into cocktail-glass.

10. New York

2 oz. Scotch Whisky
Teaspoon Unsweetened Lime Juice
Heaped teaspoon Powdered Sugar

Stir briskly, strain into cocktail-glass and squeeze Lemon rind over.

11. Rob Roy

½ Scotch Whisky
½ Sweet Vermouth

Shake, and strain into cocktail-glass.

12. Whisky Mac

Half and half Scotch Whisky and Ginger Wine
(see Chapter 18).

13. Whisky Sour

1 oz. Scotch Whisky
½ teaspoon Powdered Sugar
Juice of ½ Lemon
Teaspoon Egg White

Shake and strain into large cocktail-glass.

Another version omits Egg White and tops drink with squirt of Soda-Water.

14. Whisky Toddy

Heaped teaspoon of Sugar in warm glass; add a little boiling water and dissolve Sugar. Add 2 oz. Scotch Whisky and stir (with silver spoon). Pour in more boiling water, and top with more Scotch.

Whisky (as a traveller's aid)

A generous measure of Scotch Whisky before meals in foreign parts has been strongly recommended as 'the best possible preventative for Spanish or other tummy' by a correspondent to the *Financial Times*.

CHAPTER 6

Other Whisk(e)y

AMERICAN WHISKEY

THE LAW lists 29 types of American whiskey, but today only
the following are in commerce – straight Rye; straight Bourbon; straight Corn; blended straight Bourbon, and blended
Whiskey. Bonded (bottled in bond) whiskey is not legally
defined as a separate type.

In practice, the word 'rye' in the Eastern States is often
loosely used for whiskey which may or may not have any
particular rye base, and generic descriptions of whiskey seem
to have developed on regional historic preferences not
necessarily reflected in today's actual consumer choice. Thus,
in the South and West 'Bourbon' may be used conversation-
ally for any whiskey.

The law lays down that rye is whiskey made from a mash
containing at least 51 per cent rye: Bourbon is made from a
minimum of 51 per cent corn (maize). Both must be distilled
at not above 160 proof (US).

Bourbon is the king of American whiskey. In 1964,
Congress, in protecting the name, laid down that it is 'a
distinctive product of the United States'. The very best is
bottled in bond and will be at least four years aged in wood,
most likely considerably older.

Apart from Kentucky, Bourbon is distilled by several
companies in California, Georgia, Illinois, Indiana, Ohio and

Pennsylvania. It has a history as long as that of the United States, and a précis of this notable product's story may interest readers. In 1789, the year George Washington became first president, the Rev. Elijah Craig, a Baptist preacher of singularly catholic views, began distilling in Bourbon County, Virginia, later incorporated in Kentucky. (It appears whiskey was first distilled in America in 1640, in New York, though why the Dutch should make whiskey is not clear: I reckon it was gin.)

Within two years of the establishment of the United States, its government imposed a tax on domestic distilling, which was active. This led to the Whiskey Rebellion of 1794. That was not much of a rebellion as they go, but it widened the taste for whiskey, both through introducing it to the soldiers sent by General Washington to coerce recalcitrant distiller-farmers and by forcing some of the latter further afield where they spread the gospel according to the Rev. Craig.

Famous Bourbon Drinkers

Well-documented evidence shows that numerous American celebrities were bourbon devotees; amongst others – General Grant; Calvin Coolidge; Franklin D. Roosevelt; Davy Crockett . . . and Mark Twain. The last-named when arriving in England told the Customs Officer he had nothing to declare, his cases held only clothes. Searching, the officer found a bottle of Bourbon. 'Only clothes, sir?' he queried ironically. 'Yes', replied the famous author, 'you are holding my nightcap.'

As far as the American market goes, *Liquor Store Magazine* in a survey (1965) states that Blended whiskey is the largest selling type. Blended whiskey need not contain more than 20 per cent whiskey by volume at 100 proof, the rest being made up from neutral spirits. While these will normally be from grain, they may be made from any materials distilled at or about 190 proof (200 proof US is absolute alcohol). Neutral spirits need not be aged. While in theory a mixture of 20 per cent whiskey and 80 per cent any legal distilled spirit becomes a blend, in fact the top-selling blends are extremely carefully made, containing several whiskeys, well 'married' with grain neutral spirit and, in some cases, subsequently re-stored in cask for maturing.

Blends are consistent in flavour, while straight whiskey may vary slightly according to such factors as fluctuating conditions of the grain crop. If the product is to be labelled Blended Bourbon or Rye it must contain at least 51 per cent of those types.

American whiskey is the basis for several famous mixed drinks, and unless a type is specifically called for by tradition I am simply nominating 'whiskey'. A number of leading American brands have gained a following in Britain since the war and are sold in the better bars and stores.

Canadian Whisky

There are some twenty whisky distilleries in Canada, each producing a particular brand style. Over a century ago Canadian whisky was popular in the USA and other world markets: it retains its hold. Though using the British (Sikes) proofing system and the now traditional British spelling of the name, and although Scots played a big part in establishing the Canadian distilling industry, Canadian whisky is distinctively different from – indeed, somewhere half-way between – Scotch and American products.

Corn is the most usual basis for the mash from which Canadian whisky is distilled, plus some rye, wheat and barley malt. As in the United States, the whisky is matured in charred wood casks (the legal minimum age being two years) and is then blended to produce the delicately flavoured, mild and light-bodied characteristics of Canadian whisky.

IRISH WHISKEY

Irish whiskey is notable for the fact that the five distilleries producing it (four in Eire, one in Northern Ireland) mature their product in wood for a minimum of 7 years. This produces an exceptionally mellow spirit, and it is claimed for it that no additive whatever is required.

It is known that *Uisge Beatha* was made in Ireland at least eight hundred years ago. Not noted for his pro-Celtic leanings, Dr Samuel Johnson said of this drink that 'the Irish sort is particularly distinguished for its pleasant and mild flavour'.

Irish whiskey is made from a mash of grains, mainly barley, half of which is malted, and some wheat and oats. Use of oats is peculiar to Irish distilling. The pot-still method (as for Scottish Malts) is usual. Straight whiskies were once the rule, but Irish blends have gained a certain prominence in the United States. In England, the popularity of Irish has declined in the course of the century, but the Irish Whiskey Distillers' Association is active in promoting this famous spirit and has been particularly successful with Irish Coffee (q.v.).

'Whiskey is a bad thing – especially bad whiskey.'
Old Gaelic Saying

12. Kentucky Gentleman Bittersweet

Juice of one fresh Orange mixed with ½ teaspoon Powdered Sugar. Add 1½ oz. 'Kentucky Gentleman' Bourbon and 2 dashes of Angostura; shake and serve on to ice cubes in stemmed glass.

13. Liberal

½ Canadian Whisky
½ Sweet Vermouth
3 dashes Amer Picon
Dash Orange Bitters

 Stir, strain into cocktail-glass.

14. Manhattan

1 oz. Bourbon Whiskey
½ oz. Dry Vermouth
½ oz. Sweet Vermouth
Dash of Angostura

 Stir, strain into cocktail-glass. Serve with Cocktail Cherry.

15. Manhattan Skyscraper

Over ice in tumbler pour 2 oz. Bourbon; 1 oz. Dry Vermouth; dash of Angostura. Fill with Canada Dry Ginger Ale.

16. Millionaire

¾ Bourbon Whiskey
¼ Cointreau
Dash of Grenadine
White of an Egg

 Shake briskly, strain into large cocktail-glass.

76

COCKTAILS AND MIXED DRINKS MADE WITH AMERICAN, IRISH AND CANADIAN WHISKIES

1. Bourbon Cooler

Tall glass well-filled with cracked ice. Fill to half-way with Lime Juice; add 1 oz. Four Roses Bourbon

 Top with Pineapple Juice; stir.

2. Bourbon Fog

1 quart Strong Black Coffee, very cold
1 quart Bourbon Whiskey
1 quart Vanilla Ice-Cream

 Mix together in a punch-bowl and stir carefully.

3. Bourbon Sour

1 oz. Four Roses Bourbon
½ oz. Lemon Juice
1 teaspoon Powdered Sugar

 Shake, and strain into small tumbler.
 (See Gin Sour.)

73

4. Brainstorm

2 oz. Irish Whiskey
2 dashes Dry Vermouth
2 dashes Benedictine

Serve in small (Old Fashioned) tumbler with ice, twist of Orange peel, and stirrer.

5. Broken Leg

Stir in a suitable mug—
1 oz. Bourbon Whiskey
2½ oz. hot Apple Juice
4 Raisins
Stick of Cinnamon
Slice of Lemon.

6. Buckaroo

Into tall glass put—
1½ oz. American Whiskey
Several dashes Angostura
Several ice cubes

Top with Coca-Cola and stir.

7. Canada Cocktail

1½ oz. Canadian Whisky
2 dashes Cointreau
2 dashes Angostura
Teaspoon Powdered Sugar

Shake, strain into cocktail-glass.

8. Fancy Free

1½ oz. Rye Whiskey
Dash Orange Bitters
Dash Angostura
2 dashes Maraschino

Shake, strain into cocktail-glass whose rim has been dipped in Lemon Juice and Powdered Sugar.

9. Harrity

1 oz. Canadian Whisky
Dash of Dry Gin
Dash Angostura

Stir, strain into cocktail-glass.

10. Highball

This originally meant a tall (usually Whiskey) unflavoured spirit drink in the USA – as opposed, say, to a Julep. It is now indiscriminately used for various long iced spirit drinks topped with mineral or plain water.

11. Irish Coffee

In a stemmed glass, or small teacup, put a heaped teaspoon of Sugar (the amount depends on personal taste). Add a good measure of Irish Whiskey. Pour on Strong Hot Coffee and stir to dissolve sugar.

Cover with fresh Cream by pouring very tenderly over back of silver spoon. Serve without disturbing cream on surface.

17. Mint Julep

(There are infinite variations on this: I choose one from the Bourbon Institute's own book).
4 sprigs of Mint
1 lump Sugar
1 tablespoon water
2 oz. Bourbon Whiskey
Crushed ice

Muddle Mint, Sugar and water in tall glass. Fill with ice. Add Bourbon. Do NOT stir. Garnish with Fresh Mint sprig.

18. Old Fashioned

In small tumbler (the dumpy type that takes its name from this Cocktail)—
1 teaspoon Sugar Syrup
3 dashes Angostura
2 ice cubes
1½ oz. Bourbon Whiskey (or Rye)

Stir well, and serve with stirrer, twist of Lemon rind and Cocktail Cherry.

(Mainly associated with American Whiskey, this *may* be made with Scotch, Gin, Brandy or Rum.)

19. Pennsylvania Punch (modern version)

Juice of 12 Lemons
Quart of water
Cup of Powdered Sugar

1 bottle Bourbon
1 bottle Brandy
½ bottle Peach Brandy

Stir together with ice in punch-bowl and garnish with slices of Orange.

20. Rye and Dry (Canadian)

2 oz. Seagram's V.O. Whisky poured over ice in squat tumbler. Top with Dry Ginger Ale.

21. Sazerac

1 teaspoon Sugar Syrup
2 dashes Angostura
2 oz. American Whiskey

Stir well; strain into chilled small tumbler in which dash of Pernod has been swilled round (any surplus being tossed out).

(There are various versions of this Cocktail, and the name also belongs to a celebrated proprietary bottled Cocktail made in New Orleans for over a century.)

22. Serpent's Tooth

1 oz. Irish Whiskey
2 oz. Sweet Vermouth
1 oz. Lemon Juice
½ oz. Kummel
Dash of Angostura

Stir well, strain into small wine-glass.

23. Shamrock

½ Irish Whiskey
½ Dry Vermouth
3 dashes Green Chartreuse
3 dashes Green Crème de Menthe

Stir well, strain into cocktail-glass, serve with Green Olive.

CHAPTER 7

Vodka – A Commercial Marvel

VODKA might be said, in its Anglo-Saxon connexions, to be compounded equally of advertising, chat, fashion, fallacy and spirit! It is Russian by popular inference; the United States made it fashionable. It tastes of nothing; people laud its virtues. It contains no ingredients of medicinal merit; its consumers praise its healthfulness. It was brilliantly promoted in the USA so that despite its communistic connotations it achieved immense sales – while Americans were fighting a bitter anti-communist war in Korea.

The Russians and Poles say that what we call vodka is not vodka at all. Pedantry is perhaps on their side, but the word vodka is more generic than specific and has wide currency: for a long time it has been used in a score of countries for local distillations.

Russian and Polish vodkas have distinctive character and subtle flavours, are distilled from grain spirit, and are mellowed. They also usually cost more, and deserve to be treated correctly. That is, one takes them severely chilled in small glasses, straight, to the accompaniment preferably of caviar but certainly with some tasty morsels of smoked fish or similar titbit. (There is no need to crash the empty glass into the fireplace, but the desire to perform this semi-traditional and satisfying ritual will increase in proportion to the intake of neat spirit!)

It is a waste of fine drink to use imported vodkas, which

have a comparatively small but steady sale amongst informed imbibers, for Cocktails, nor are they designed for drinking with mineral additives. Conversely, British-made vodkas lack the character to make them suitable as a straight drink for the discerning; they are intended to put zest into mixed drinks.

Vodka is becoming increasingly popular in Britain: whether this drink will achieve the extraordinary vogue it has in the USA remains to be seen. I doubt it, yet as a commercial proposition it is nothing short of miraculous, and vodka's story is worth tracing if only for that reason.

Encyclopaedic references tend to perpetuate the legend that vodka is made from potatoes. One can make excellent spirit from that vegetable source, but I doubt if any serious vodka, domestic or foreign (and vodka is produced in many countries) is thus made today. It will almost certainly be based on grain or cane spirit.

The greater *Oxford English Dictionary* spells vodka nine different ways and describes it as 'an ardent spirit'. It has a legendary origin in 12th century Russia, and the word itself can literally be translated as 'little water'. The Poles also claim to have invented it. Probably it started as a botanically-flavoured medicine. In due course vodka also became the national drink of Finland, the Baltic states, and spread as far afield as Persia.

Inventive Czar

Peter the Great took an interest in distilling, and that ever-curious tyrant invented a formula, called after him 'Petrovskaya', which is the basis of Russian vodka today. In 1895, the Czar made vodka distilling into a State monopoly and during the first World War banned distillation completely. This prohibition was maintained by the Soviets until 1925, when it was realized that illicit distilling was rife and drunkenness a national scandal – as it always is when there is Prohibition. Legal manufacture by the State was reintroduced. The vodka question, as a social problem, crops up from time to time in the USSR. Finland, too, had a lot of trouble with alcoholism induced by Prohibition, and now exercises stringent State control: the monopoly produces excellent vodka which is sold through a somewhat crazy rationing system.

The modern march of vodka in the United States started in the late forties when Heublein's, who had acquired the brand name of a famous vodka from its owners, found a small sale for it in California where it was drunk with iced ginger-beer. This was the birth of the Moscow Mule. Some unsung advertising genius cooked up the slogan 'leaves you breathless', which is ambiguous enough but which drinkers chose to take as meaning you could drink vodka and it would not be noticed. This, to my mind, fallacious notion did wonders. Sales rose, more advertising money was available, and a repetition of this process quickly brought about something near a revolution in American drinking patterns. Admittedly, there was a steady rise in all drink sales – yet that of vodka was meteoric. The Vodkatini was born – which I consider a sad bastardization of the Dry Martini Cocktail (q.v.) – and the Bloody Mary (an excellent pick-me-up and truly a vodka drink) was rediscovered.

This craze, as is the wont of American habits, soon crossed the Atlantic and the owners of the British rights to the same brand as had spurted in the US got a head start. As in the USA, they now have plenty of competitors.

Vodka (Anglo-American style) is simply a pure spirit that is filtered through a special form of charcoal to render it palatable. That is about all there is to it. It is usually sold at 65·5 proof, against the normal 70 proof of whisky, gin or brandy.

Stronger domestic vodkas are made, retailing proportionately higher, and are imported – including the immensely powerful Polish Pure Spirit.

Zubrowka vodka is also available; it is flavoured with, and coloured pale green by, the infusion of zubrowka grass. Some authorities hold this not to be a vodka but correctly a 'gin'. I cannot concede this: Gin must contain juniper. In the Leningrad vodka factory, about thirty types of flavoured vodka are produced, for regional demand, with flavourings ranging from sugar to red pepper. They are certainly vodkas. Russian vodkas from the Ukraine, Lithuania and Latvia are occasionally available in Britain. The imported market is dominated by two brands, Polish (Vyborova) and Russian (Stolichnaya). The domestic market is led by Smirnoff and 'Cossack' brands – with some other names getting in on a rising tide.

> 'Free yourself from the slavery of tea and coffee and other slopkettle.'
>
> *William Cobbett*

DRINKS ESSENTIALLY ASSOCIATED WITH VODKA

1. Balalaika

$\frac{1}{2}$ Vodka
$\frac{1}{4}$ Lemon Juice
$\frac{1}{4}$ Cointreau

Shake, and strain into cocktail-glass. Serve with a twist of Orange peel.

2. Barbara

1 oz. Vodka
½ oz. Crème de Cacao
½ oz. fresh Cream

Shake well, and strain into cocktail-glass.

3. Blenheim

½ Vodka
¼ Tia Maria
¼ fresh Orange Juice

Shake, and strain into cocktail-glass.

4. Bloody Mary

See Chapter 17.

5. Bogey

2 oz. 'Cossack' Vodka over ice cubes in pint tankard; 1 oz. Lime Juice Cordial; top with Ginger-Beer and decorate with slice of Lemon.

J. and J. Vickers & Co.

6. Bull Shot

See Chapter 17.

7. Chelsea Reach

2 oz. 'Cossack' Vodka poured over ice cubes in tall glass; add 2 oz. Jaffa Juice (or good quality Orange Squash); top with Medium-Dry Cider.

Miss M. J. Wallis

8. Cossack Cooler

A good measure of 'Cossack' Vodka over ice cubes in tall glass. Fill with equal amounts Ginger Ale and Medium-Dry Cider. Garnish with slice of Lemon. (When available, rub rim of glass with Fresh Mint.)

J. and J. Vickers & Co.

9. Gipsy

⅔ Vodka
⅓ Benedictine
Dash Angostura
   Shake, strain into cocktail-glass.

10. Iceberg

   Pour 2 oz. Vodka over ice cubes in small tumbler. Add dash of Pernod. Stir.

11. Muscovital

1 oz. Vodka
2 oz. Crabbie's Green Ginger Wine
1 oz. Campari

   Mix with ice in tumbler and serve with Cocktail Cherry.

12. Screwdriver

2 oz. Vodka
1 oz. Orange Juice
½ teaspoon Powdered Sugar

   Shake, strain into medium-size glass. Add ice and a slice of Orange.

85

13. Summertime

Over ice cubes in tall glass pour 1 oz. Vodka, 1 oz. Dry Vermouth, Juice of ½ Grapefruit. Top with Canada Dry Tonic-Water.

14. Twister

1½ oz. Vodka
Teaspoon Unsweetened (or Fresh) Lime Juice

Pour over ice cubes in tall glass; top with '7-Up'.

15. Vodkatini

As for a Dry Martini, but a piece of Lemon peel immersed may be in order to give the Vodka character. Do not confuse with a true Dry Martini (see Chapter 3).

CHAPTER 8

Rum – A Question
of Contrast

IT WOULD be simple to say that rum is a spirit distilled from
sugar-cane residue, and that it has widespread application in
the world of Mixed Drinks.

However, rum shows more marked differences of flavour
according to its origin than any spirit in general use. One may
have relished real Navy rum, rich and powerful, which some
connoisseurs claim to be the only real rum there is. One has
probably tasted, straight or in a mixed drink, the very light
Cuban rum. Both are true rums, yet they could hardly contrast more decisively. So we must give a short explanation of
the various types of rum, before discovering the famous
drinks that may be made from them.

Rum has for long been produced in all sugar-producing
countries, and in some areas, notably New England, where
the raw material must be imported. (There is also a considerable distillation from molasses in England for the production
of a neutral spirit widely used in making vodka and gins. But
this is not rum.)

In the mid-seventeenth century raw spirit was produced
in the British West Indies, but this was chiefly a stimulant
for slaves, and it appears it was some time before refinements
led to the production of true rum. It became the traditional
drink of British seafarers, and very popular with the working

classes. While used by rich planters, it did not enjoy much social acceptance in Britain until its value in mixed drinks came to sophisticated attention. While there is a regionally varying demand for the heavier rums, it is on the whole the lighter ones which are making progress today in the context of this book.

Jamaica rum is usually pungent, although they do produce lighter ones as well. The Jamaican type is that traditionally associated with the word rum in Britain.

Barbados and Trinidad rums are light and dry.

Demerara rum (from Guyana) tends to be dark and rather heavy, but less pungent than Jamaican.

Cuban rum is light in colour and flavour. The best known brand, Bacardi, is now made outside Cuba for obvious reasons, while from Guyana (associated with dark rums) comes the ultra-light Daiquiri*, successful and less expensive British competitor to Bacardi, as is Tropicana.

Rum is brought into England in bottle, and in bulk for maturing and bottling here, and the latter has prestige as a re-export. Apart from 'Cuban', I do not know of any important import of non-British rums. The Caribbean, parts of Central and South America, Australia and South Africa also produce large quantities of rum, mainly for local use, though the USA imports a good deal of 'Cuban' rum from Puerto Rico and some from her Virgin Islands as these, through preferential tariffs, can compete with non-American brands.

Rum benefits from long maturing in wood, and twelve and twenty-year-old rums are not uncommon. No rums under three years may be sold in Britain.

Where the word rum came from is not known. It is attributed to 'Rumbullion', a Devon word, and Devonians were great explorers. *Saccharum*, Latin for sugar, is another theory.

At the time of writing the registration of 'Daiquiri' as a brand-name is in dispute.

The Spanish call it *ron*, and the French drink a lot of aromatic *rhum* from their West Indies possessions.

> 'Man wants but little drink below,
> But wants that little strong.'
>
> *O. W. Holmes*

MIXED DRINKS WITH RUM

1. Apple Rum Punch

Take 6 fresh Oranges and stick them with 10 Cloves apiece. Bake until rind browned. Put into punch-bowl, which should be warm, and add 1 bottle mellow Rum; ½ bottle Brandy and 4 tablespoons Sugar. Stir well. Set the mixture alight. Extinguish with 3 bottles of Shloer Apple Juice. Sprinkle with Ground Cinnamon and Grated Nutmeg and serve warm in teacups or glasses with handles.

2. Bacardi Cocktail*

½ 'Bacardi' Rum
¼ Lemon Juice or Lime Juice
¼ Grenadine

Shake well, strain into cocktail-glass.

3. Captain's Blood

1½ oz. Mellow Rum
2 teaspoons Unsweetened Lime Juice
Dash of Angostura

Shake briskly, strain into cocktail-glass.

4. Cuba Libre

2 oz. Light Rum
Tablespoon Unsweetened (preferably Fresh) Lime Juice

Pour over ice in tall glass. Top with Coca-Cola and add twist of Lime or Lemon rind.

5. Daiquiri*

Traditionally—
$\frac{1}{2}$ 'Bacardi' Rum
$\frac{1}{4}$ fresh Lime Juice
$\frac{1}{4}$ Grenadine
Shaken and strained; served very cold.

But Lemon may now replace Lime, and Sugar the Grenadine.

*Is also known as Bacardi Cocktail, as there is now an excellent rum called Daiquiri. (See footnote to p. 88.)

6. Fish House Punch

2 bottles Jamaica Rum
1 bottle Brandy
$\frac{3}{4}$ lb. Brown Sugar
3 pints water
2 teaspoons Peach Bitters

Blend very thoroughly and pour over large lump of ice in big bowl.

(This is only one version of a famous American Punch said to be originated in Philadelphia in the early 18th century.)

7. Planters' Punch

2 oz. 'Myers' Rum
1 oz. Lemon Juice
Teaspoon Grenadine
Dash Angostura

Stir with plenty of ice in tall glass. Add more crushed ice and top with Soda-Water. Decorate with rounds of Lemon and Orange. Serve with straws.

8. Riviera

½ 'Bacardi' Rum
¼ Cointreau
¼ Regnier Framboise (raspberry)

Mix with ice in tumbler; top with Bitter-Lemon and squeeze over it quarter of a Fresh Lemon which is left in the drink.

9. Rum Nogg

1½ oz. Dark Rum
1 Egg
1 level teaspoon Powdered Sugar
⅔ pint Milk

Shake thoroughly, strain into tall glass.
Add a little Grated Nutmeg.

10. Silverstone

Equal proportions White Rum and Martini Bianco.

Stir with ice; add a little Bitter-Lemon.
  Martini & Rossi

11. Spanish Captain

⅔ 'Myers' Rum
⅓ Dry Sherry
Teaspoon Lime Juice

Shake, and strain into cocktail-glass, serving with a Cherry.
House of Seagram

12. Tea Punch

½ bottle Jamaica Rum
½ bottle Cognac
½ lb. Sugar Syrup
1 quart Strong Tea
A large Lemon

Heat a metal punch-bowl, and into it put the Brandy, Rum, Sugar and Juice of the Lemon. (Rub lumps of Sugar on the rind of the Lemon and add these to the mixture.) Set contents of bowl on fire, and gradually add the Hot Tea.

13. Tom and Jerry

Beat separately the Yolks and Whites of a dozen Eggs. Beat ½ lb. Sugar into Yolks together with tablespoon each of Powdered Cinnamon, Cloves and Allspice. Pour in 6 oz. Dark Jamaica Rum, stirring all the time, and then fold in Whites and put aside. Put a generous serving into mug of about ⅓ pint capacity, add 2 oz. Bourbon (or Scotch or Irish), fill with boiling water and/or Milk, stirring vigorously, and top with Grated Nutmeg.

Adapted from recipe of
Mr D. A. Embury

14. Trader Vic's Punch

1¼ oz. Light Rum
1¼ oz. Dark Jamaica Rum
½ an Orange
½ a Lemon
1 slice Pineapple
Teaspoon Sugar
½ teaspoon Orgeat Syrup (optional in UK: Grenadine may be used)

Squeeze Orange and Lemon and drop in mixer; add ice and remainder ingredients. Shake briskly, pour unstrained into tall glass. Serve with straws.

Trader Vic

CHAPTER 9

Brandy – Vive La France

BRANDY is spirit distilled from grapes or wine. It is made in all wine-producing countries, and there are brandies produced from other fruit bases. However, when you use the word, it is ten-to-one you are speaking of COGNAC. That comes only from France (though the Spaniards label brandy *coñac*). No spirit that does not come from the designated area may in France be named cognac and this condition is acknowledged virtually internationally.

Cognac is an ancient town on the Charente, a little north of Bordeaux. For a brandy to justify the designation cognac it must be made from wine coming from eight legally specified types of grape, grown within a carefully mapped area, and distillation must be by pot-still according to precisely defined methods.

You may have noticed that the best cognacs carry the description Fine Champagne, which I think very few people today confuse in any way with the famous wine. This means simply that it is a mixture of distillations from the two most coveted districts (the *Grande* and *Petite* Champagne). There are five other areas, of descending prestige.

Though drunk locally, the wines of the Cognac district are harsh and are cultivated almost wholly for distillation. They are produced by farmers who, in the *Grande* and *Petite* Champagne, have possibly the most valuable land in the world, not forgetting Manhattan, and certainly the most valuable agricultural land. Distillation takes place intensively over a season of some six months and under strict governmental supervision.

The spirit is matured in casks of untreated oak from the nearby forests of Limousin. Through evaporation and other causes, there is an annual loss of spirit in cask of some 3 per cent though this varies according to conditions of storage. Cognacs on the market are all blended. There is a good deal of confusion about age of cognacs, which can only be expressed in averages. The 'star' system, dropped by several brands, indicates nothing much. Where used, '3 star' means a sound normal-priced cognac of about 5 years. (In France in 1939 I bought a very ordinary cognac bearing nine stars: it was as phoney as the war then in progress!) The leading brands have their commercial grade, plus several other older and more costly ones.

The designations you are most likely to encounter are 'Three Star'; VSOP (Very Superior Old Pale – it was once usual to drink dark-coloured cognac in England, but then fashion changed; hence this styling); and XO (Extra Old). There are various other trade stylings for quality, Bras Armé, etc., plus brands' own names for aged, often called 'Liqueur', cognacs such as the well-known *Cordon Bleu* and *Médaillon*. A cognac may carry an actual date, but this should not be taken too literally. It may represent spirit from the 'oldest' cask in the blend.

Don't Go Nap On This!

Beware the abused 'Napoleon' (which refers not to Bonaparte but to Napoleon III) title, which should be only an indication that a proportion of very old brandy is in the blend. However, I have before me a wine list featuring a 'Napoleon 3 Star'! There is altogether too much snobbery about 'Napoleon

Brandy'; but do not take this as a reflection on the merit of the respected slogan 'the brandy of Napoleon' (Bonaparte) used by Courvoisier. Cognac matured and bottled in France may not carry an indication of a 'Year', but spirit shipped to Britain from France a year after the vintage from which it was distilled, and bottled after long maturing in this country, may, for exceptionally fine cognacs, carry a date.

Rare and costly cognacs are to be treated with great respect, drunk from a brandy 'snifter' of reasonable size so that it may comfortably be warmed by the hand. Exaggeratedly large brandy glasses are an affectation objectionable to connoisseurs, and wasteful, and the practice of crudely heating the glass in a flame – there are even vulgar instruments sold for this purpose – is to be condemned. Half the joy in fine cognac comes from slowly inhaling the unique bouquet, gently coaxed from the spirit, before letting the palate participate.

The sound ordinary brands of commerce are hardly suitable for this ritual treatment, and it is no desecration to drink them with additives or in the excellent cocktails that may be brandy-based.

The British, for long great consumers of French brandies, have for generations been associated with cognac. The Martells came from the Channel Islands; the Hennessys from Ireland; the Hines (correctly pronounced with an 'H' and not Frenchified to 'een') from the West of England.

Normally, cognac in Britain is sold at 70 proof, as for other spirits, with de luxe brands often stronger, and in bottles of 24 fluid ounces in place of the usual 26⅔.

Apart From Cognac

The other great name in French brandy is ARMAGNAC, of

which long-aged ones are prized by a few experts even beyond cognac. This distinctive brandy is produced under strict control in the region of that name, well south of Cognac, to the West of Toulouse. Production is about a quarter that of cognac, and unlike that spirit, which is double-distilled, armagnac comes from a single distillation of the wine and requires considerably longer in wood; twenty years is quite normal. It is commercially available in Britain and sold by competent wine merchants and in the more sophisticated or specialized bars and restaurants.

Though very little drunk in Britain, or indeed outside France, CALVADOS brandy, distilled in Normandy from apples (Normandy is a great cider producing area, which is said to be the reason for the notoriously bad teeth of its inhabitants) is at its best highly esteemed by those who know it. The same spirit in the USA is called applejack. When aged a great time, it is a remarkable spirit. I once drank a calvados which had rested ninety years in cask and it was a memorable experience: this had not been made for selling but for private stock. I would say there rest distinct possibilities in marketing this admirable brandy in Britain; but some local distillations can be pretty rough.

There are those who relish the various *marcs* (pronounced 'mar') distilled from fermented residue of grapes after wine pressings or from poor or surplus wine. Perhaps the *Marc de Bourgogne* is the best known and can be of high quality. But the *marc* one purchases in a *bistro* may sear the throat. What is simply referred to in France as *eau-de-vie* is normally a rather rough *marc*.

Other Brandies

Many holiday-makers have come across the brandies of other countries. That of Spain – pleasantly pungent – I find delightful when drunk in that country, but, as is often the case with potables, less satisfactory in Britain. German and Italian brandies are, at their best, also excellent, more aromatic than cognac, and there are those who like *grappa* which is the Italian equivalent of the French *marc*. Greek brandy, smooth and of very pronounced flavour, can also be pleasing, though I personally would add the same qualification as for Spanish.

It would be quite impossible to list the grape brandies of the world, but it is worth mentioning that California produces more brandy than France. South African and Cypriot brandies, obtainable in Britain, are adequate for some Cocktails. Australia is another huge producer of brandy, and I have heard travellers say kind things about some Russian brandies.

Other brandies which you may come across, but which have little relevance to this book, are *Slivovitz* (from plums), sometimes called *Quetsch*; *Kirsch* (from cherries), widely esteemed; *Raki* (or *Rakia*), from wine or other materials, and sundry brandies of many flavours of little or no merit or not easily available in Britain. 'Cherry Brandy' is a pleasing drink, but, as opposed to *Kirsch*, is not a brandy but a cordial liqueur.

It is commonly thought the word brandy derives from the Dutch *brandewijn*: 'burnt' (i.e. distilled) wine'. *Brandewine* was used in the 17th century in England, not necessarily for brandy but for various distillations. It seems likely, however, that, becoming *Brandywine*, and shortened to 'Brandy', at a date unknown in the 18th century, the term began to be applied to imported French grape spirit and afterwards to similar spirits.

As in the case of all spirits, brandy in no way improves in glass: with cognac or armagnac, it is not the dust on the bottle that counts but the time its contents spent in the cask.

'A mixture of brandy and water spoils two good things.'
Charles Lamb

DRINKS BASED ON BRANDIES

1. Alexander

⅓ Cognac
⅓ Crème de Càcao
⅓ Fresh Cream

Shake thoroughly, and strain into cocktail-glass.

2. American Beauty

¼ Brandy
1 dash Crème de Menthe
¼ Orange Juice
¼ Grenadine
¼ Dry Vermouth

Shake, strain into wine-glass. Top with a little Port.

3. Applejack Rabbit

1½ oz. Calvados
½ Lemon Juice
½ Orange Juice
Teaspoon Grenadine Syrup

Shake, strain into cocktail-glass.

4. Betsy Ross

1 oz. Brandy
1 oz. Port
Dash Angostura
½ teaspoon Cointreau (or less)

  Shake, strain into cocktail-glass.

5. Bonnie Prince Charlie

1 oz. Brandy
½ oz. Drambuie
1 oz. Lemon Juice

  Shake, strain into cocktail-glass.

6. Booster Cocktail

2 oz. Brandy
Teaspoon Cointreau
White of 1 Egg

  Shake, and strain into medium-size glass.
  Grated Nutmeg on top.

7. Brandy Daisy

2 oz. Brandy
Juice of 1 Lemon
½ oz. Grenadine

  Mix well with cracked ice, pour unstrained into goblet.
  Add Cocktail Cherries. Serve with straws.

8. Brandy Cocktail

1½ oz. Cognac
1 oz. Cointreau
½ teaspoon Sugar Syrup
2 dashes Angostura

Stir briskly, strain into cocktail-glass.

9. Brandy Crusta

Moisten edge of glass with Lemon and frost with Powdered Sugar. Cut the rind of a Lemon in a spiral; place in glass, hooking over rim. Fill glass with cracked ice.
¾ Brandy
3 dashes Maraschino
¼ Cointreau
1 dash Angostura Bitters
4 dashes Lemon Juice

Stir well, strain into glass; add slice of Orange.

10. Brandy Fix

1 teaspoon Powdered Sugar dissolved in sufficient water
Juice of ½ Lemon
1 oz. Brandy
1 oz. Cherry Brandy

Mix in small tumbler, adding cracked ice. Finish with slice of Lemon. Serve with straws.

11. Brandy Hum

Equal measures South African Brandy and Van der Hum liqueur.

Could, of course, be taken 'on the rocks'.

12. Brandy Smash

Crush good-sized sprig of Mint into teaspoon Powdered Sugar in tumbler.
Add 1½ oz. Hennessy Cognac
Ice

Top with Soda-Water.
Stir.

13. Epee

¾ Cognac
¼ Martini Sweet Vermouth

Stir well and strain into cocktail-glass.

14. First Night

½ Martell Cognac
¼ Van Der Hum
¼ Tia Maria
Teaspoon fresh Cream

Shake well, and strain into cocktail-glass.
Matthew Clark and Sons

15. Grenadier

1 oz. Cognac
1 oz. Crabbie's Green Ginger Wine
1 teaspoon Powdered Sugar

Shake well, and strain into cocktail-glass.

16. Ice Cap

1 oz. Bisquit Cognac
$\frac{3}{4}$ oz. Crème de Càcao
1 tablespoon Fresh Cream

Shake thoroughly, and strain into small wine-glass or tumbler.

House of Seagram

17. Klondike

1$\frac{1}{2}$ oz. Calvados
1 oz. Dry Vermouth
2 dashes Angostura

Shake briskly, strain into cocktail-glass.

18. Netherlands

1 oz. Brandy
$\frac{1}{2}$ oz. Cointreau
Dash Orange Bitters

Stir, strain into cocktail-glass.

19. Royal Wedding

¼ Kirsch
½ Orange Juice
¼ Peach Brandy

Shake well, and strain into wine goblet. Top up with Champagne.
Savoy

20. Sidecar

½ Brandy
¼ Lemon Juice
¼ Cointreau

Shake, strain into cocktail-glass.

21. Stinger

2 oz. Brandy
1 oz. White Crème de Menthe

Shake well, strain into adequate cocktail-glass.

22. Sundowner

1 oz. South African Brandy
¼ oz. each—
Lemon Juice
Orange Juice
Van der Hum Liqueur

Shake briskly, strain into cocktail-glass.

23. Yankee Invigorator

Beat up an Egg in a shaker. Add ¾ pint Strong Cold Coffee; 1 oz. Brandy; ½ wine-glass of robust Port; Sugar to taste. Add plenty of ice.

Shake well, and strain into large tumbler.

CHAPTER 10

Other Spirits

THE minor potable spirits of the world are uncounted and uncountable. However, at least one fresh one has found its way into use in the United States, and slightly in Britain – whence the vogue might spread more widely, since these countries are pace-makers in the world of mixed drinks. Others again may be encountered on one's travels, or may be read about in books so that, without expecting to savour them, one may wish to know of what they consist. Any vegetable matter can be turned into a mash containing alcohol and from this can be distilled spirit. A country will tend naturally to use for its traditional spirits that base which is in greatest supply, be it potatoes, sugar, grapes, bananas, cereals, or whatever. Only for major potable industries, where such exist, or for sophisticated spirits, where such are in demand, will raw materials be worth importing.

TEQUILA, the Mexican spirit, is enjoying a small craze in the United States and is now on sale in Britain. Tequila is distilled from the national drink *Pulque*, the fermented sap of the maguey plant, a slow-growing cactus-like vegetable. It is a refined type of *mescal*, a fiery Mexican spirit which contains hallucinationary properties. Tequila itself enjoyed a reputation as a blockbuster, but appears to have been tamed as far as reputable brands are concerned. It is traditionally drunk thus: You require salt, a slice of lemon and a small glass of iced straight tequila. Pour some salt on to the back of your hand;

lick this off with your tongue. Squeeze some drops of lemon juice on top of this, and then toss off the tequila. Repeat until you start pouring the salt into your lap.

AQUAVIT (or similar spellings) is a generic term for the spirits, flavoured or unflavoured, of varied types, drunk in Scandinavia. The name obviously comes from that common old Latin source, *aqua vitae*. This is the Schnapps of Germany and several other countries, and covers a multitude of spirits and brands of spirit which are normally drunk neat and chilled, often accompanied by lager beer.

ABSINTHE, the drink of the original Bohemians of Paris, is no longer legally made in Switzerland, where it was invented, nor France. It was held that the wormwood that is a crucial ingredient is poisonous and habit-forming. But wormwood has long been recognized as medicinal: more likely it was the great strength of absinthe that did the damage and caused its ill-repute. It is made in some countries, with a smaller than formerly wormwood content. In the days of my youth, in the Parisian Latin Quarter one could find illicitly imported absinthe. After he had drunk four glasses of this, I recall helping to carry home the totally inert form of a student friend. We thought he had died, but after three days' sleep he was as right as rain. He was much later to gain fame as Dr Stephen Ward.

The famous PERNOD – that some call absinthe, which it is not – is strong and has many of the properties of absinthe without the wormwood. If you adore aniseed, it is a fine drink, and one can have the fun of watching it cloud as water is added: this seems to fascinate people. OJEN (oh-hen) and OUZO are respectively the Spanish and Greek equivalents.

ARRACK is the traditional spirit of the former British and Dutch Orient, and is made by distilling Toddy which is fermented sap from palm trees. A superior Dutch form is made from sugar cane and rice. Arrack is also made from coconut juice, and mare's milk. I do not think anyone would drink arrack who could obtain alternative stimulant.

AGUARDIENTE may be, generically, applied to such spirits as tequila; but on its own it is the name for raw, unmatured, spirits distilled from grapes or molasses in Spain, Portugal, the Philippines, and Central and South America. The word means 'Burning water' and, with rare exceptions, is held to be only too descriptive.

Before anyone can tell me, I know SAKE is not a spirit but a brew, sometimes called a 'wine'. However, it deserves mention as the national drink of Japan – and, under other names, of the Chinese. It is basically fermented rice, briefly mellowed and then clarified: the strength approximates to that of Vermouth. In our current Ice Age, speaking drinkwise, Sake is notable for being drunk warmed.

The All Nippon Bartenders' Association have come up with a couple of Sake cocktails, but I won't give you the one which requires the fin of a special fish. Another is called 'Tamago-zake'—

6 oz. Sake
I Egg
I teaspoon Sugar

Boil the Sake and set it alight. Immediately remove from heat, and stir in Egg and Sugar. Pour into suitable handled vessel.

This is the only *boiled* cocktail in my repertoire.

'Absinthe makes the heart grow fonder.'
Addison Mizner

OTHER DRINKS BASED ON UNCONVENTIONAL SPIRITS

1. Absinthe Cocktail

½ Absinthe*
½ Water
1 dash Sugar Syrup
1 dash Angostura Bitters

Shake, strain into cocktail-glass.
(*if you can get it.)

2. Grigio-Verde

½ Grappa*
½ Crème de Menthe
Stir, strain into cocktail-glass.
(*see Chapter 9)
   Italian Bartenders' Assn

3. Jarana

2 oz. Tequila Sauza
2 oz. Powdered Sugar

Pour over plenty of ice into tall glasses and fill with Pineapple Juice.

4. Kiss Me Quick

1½ oz. Pernod
4 dashes Cointreau
2 dashes Angostura

Shake well, strain into tall goblet. Add more ice, top with Soda-Water. Stir gently.

(This title must be a joke: the drink is not recommended for pre-osculatory use unless proposed partner also partaking.)

5. Red Viking

⅓ Akvavit
⅓ Maraschino
⅓ Lime Juice Cordial

Served 'on the rocks'.
Danish Bartenders' Institute

CHAPTER 11

Vermouth – Aperitif Wines – Bitters

VERMOUTH is imported in great quantities into Britain. Italy is its birthplace and France its second home. Nearly everyone knows that 'French' is pale and dry and 'Italian' is red and sweetish. 'Bianco' has gained recent popularity: this is paler and sweeter than the red variety. The terms 'French' and 'Italian' no longer have any geographical significance. Vermouth of both basic types is made in most wine-producing countries, and in a number of others as well, including Britain. Vermouth is not a protected name. Quality may vary considerably. Of drinks that are extremely popular, probably less is known about vermouth than about any other by the general public. Formulae are very closely guarded secrets and within a given type there is, in a similar quality bracket, considerable variation in taste. The trade is dominated by a few famous names – some countries favouring ones little considered in others – and you would do well to find the ones you like best and stick to them.

Vermouth plays a major role in Cocktails, and we should probe a little further into the subject.

Aromatic wines, with herbs and spices added, were known and appreciated in ancient civilizations. While it cannot be claimed as vermouth as we know it, there appears more than a casual resemblance to vermouth in what the Romans knew as *vinum Hippocratium*, said to have been invented in Greece by Hippocrates in the 5th century BC. In the Middle Ages the range of herbal wines increased, but it appears that vermouth as such was first commercially produced, in Italy, in the late 18th century by Giuseppe Carpano. However, the name is German by origin, though it is said it was an Italian who invented it. Whatever the facts may be, it was in Germany that *wermutwein* (wine flavoured principally with wormwood, a highly regarded medicine) first came to light. The inventor, who, Martini & Rossi tell me, was a Signor Alessio, came from Piedmont where the great city of Turin is the world's vermouth capital to this day. Alessio apparently went from Germany to Paris where the French, and then the Italians changed *Wermut* to *Vermout*. The English, with their talent for linguistic distortion, duly inserted a superfluous 'h'. By the 1880s, vermouth, principally 'Italian' (Cinzano, as now, being a leading brand), had gained world-wide support; the drier types came into prominence later. The popularity of vermouth certainly helped gin towards international social acceptance.

Briefly, vermouth is wine that has infused into it a considerable number of herbs and spices that may far exceed two dozen, and is fortified with grape brandy. The greatest care is needed to maintain continuity of flavour in a given brand, and the clarification and filtering of the product are of the greatest importance and form a long and costly process in the case of the top quality vermouth. Substitute vermouths are not necessarily based on wine at all.

Other Aperitif Wines

The best known 'aperitifs' are mainly based on vermouth or something very similar (since there is no definition of what constitutes vermouth in the way there is of, say, cognac).

These aperitifs are usually known by their trade brand-names. Many of them basically vary from accepted vermouth in having quinine as an ingredient.

CAMPARI (which is sometimes classed, wrongly I believe, as a bitters) is very sharp in an exciting way. DUBONNET is bland and smooth. FERNET-BRANCA (see Chapter 17). ST RAPHAEL is typical of French aperitifs, sweetish. BYRRH is a household name in France now growing in Britain (be careful to add 'aperitif' after the name when ordering or you will probably get a pint of bitter!). AMER PICON is another sharp-tasting wine. CHAMBERY is possibly a real vermouth, but I consider it a subtly distinctive, very dry aperitif: none too widely available in Britain. LILLET is bitter-sweet. PUNT E MES is a de luxe slightly 'bittered' dry vermouth from Italy. I think that is representative enough a list.

The French, whose liking for sweet drinks is much more marked than their presumed reputation as *bons vivants* suggests – witness that awful sticky champagne they often serve as a *vin d'honneur* (*vin d'horreur?*) – are very fond of 'Vermouth Cassis', sweet vermouth with blackcurrant cordial; which is one fashion I don't see catching on here. In Britain, the habit is growing, with young people specially, to take vermouth and similar wines straight or 'on the rocks', or with soda and lemon, or mixed (dry and sweet, preferably iced). Other than the Americano – a Negroni (q.v.) without the gin – there are, in my vocabulary, few celebrated Cocktails which, as well as vermouth, do not contain other dominant ingredients. These important wines feature plentifully in recipes under other sections, but I will enter some hereunder.

Bitters

As bitters play an important part in numerous Cocktails, this would seem an appropriate place to deal with them. I am referring to what we usually call bitters in Britain, powerful and concentrated alcoholic infusions of various ingredients, not made for drinking on their own but as zestful additions to other drinks.

By far the best known are ANGOSTURA, favoured all over the world, originally compounded by Dr J. G. B. Siegert, an army surgeon, in 1824 Angostura, a village in what is now Venezuela. Later the commercialization of this product was moved to Trinidad. Angostura is, of course, what makes Pink Gin pink (see gin recipes). My personal theory on the origin of this drink, publicly propounded during a lively correspondence in the *Daily Telegraph* in the course of 1965, is that angostura bitters were once used as an anti-fever and -scurvy specific in the Royal Navy. Rather too sharp to be taken undiluted with any pleasure, and old-time shipboard water being what it was, resource was had to taking the bitters with spirit. Brandy, the most probable drink of officers, or the official rum, would not be entirely suitable. It would be natural for a ship coming from Plymouth, or London for that matter, to have taken on gin. Some unknown Naval experimenter may have tried mixing angostura bitters and gin. Eureka! And so a new mixed drink was born.

Orange bitters are compounded of quinine, orange oil, spirit and other ingredients. The other ones in fairly general use are the altogether milder peach bitters. But it's Angostura that's a necessity for a bar, domiciliary or professional.

I was amused to discover that, contrary to British practice, in the United States potions there classified as bitters, despite their frequently high alcoholic content, do not attract federal excise tax for medicinal or other reasons. If such a ruling applied here, perhaps we'd be able to make a case for an interesting range of exemptions: gin, vermouth, Angostura,

Pernod ... a lot of spirituous beverages have therapeutic agents in them!

> 'I'm quite in favour of temperance propaganda, providing it doesn't unduly restrict the sale of intoxicating liquor.'
> *St J. Hankin*

SOME MIXED DRINKS OWING A LOT TO THEIR APERITIF CONTENT

1. Americano

⅔ Sweet Vermouth
⅓ Campari
Lump of ice

Pour over ice in large wine-glass. Fill with Soda, stir, and add a twist of Lemon peel and dash of Angostura.

2. Bamboo

¼ Dry Vermouth
¼ Sweet Vermouth
½ Dry Sherry

Stir well, strain into cocktail-glass.

3. Bentley

½ Calvados
½ Dubonnet

Shake well, and strain into cocktail-glass.
Savoy

4. Byrrh Cocktail

⅓ Byrrh
⅓ Dry Vermouth
⅓ Rye Whiskey

Stir, strain into cocktail-glass.

5. Coronation

1 oz. each—
Dry Vermouth
Dubonnet
Dry Gin

Stir, strain into cocktail-glass.

6. Count Rossi

In small tumbler—
2 ice cubes

Top with half-and-half Martini & Rossi Sweet and Dry Vermouth. Squeeze Lemon rind over; serve with slice of Orange.

7. Dubonnet Cocktail

½ Dubonnet
½ Dry Gin

Stir, strain into cocktail-glass.

8. Kitty Love

⅓ Cointreau
⅓ Kirsch
⅓ Carpano
2 dashes Orange Juice

Shake, strain into cocktail-glass; garnish with Orange rind.
Luxembourg Bartenders' Union

9. Perfect Cocktail

⅓ Dry Vermouth
⅓ Sweet Vermouth
⅓ Dry Gin

Shake, strain into cocktail-glass.

10. Vermouth Cassis

2 oz. Dry Vermouth (or Sweet)
½ oz. Cassis (Blackcurrant Cordial)

Pour over ice in tumbler; add splash of Soda-Water.
(Traditional French aperitif drink.)

CHAPTER 12

Table Wines – Some Matters of Opinion

IT CAN be described as 'Marcobrunner Riesling Trocken-beerenauslese Cabinet' or 'Chilean Burgundy': it is all wine. Wines have their place in this book, for they can form the basis of a number of interesting mixed drinks of diverse complexity; but the subject is immense and by no feat of compression could I give a background to wine nor even my own small store of knowledge of it. Wine of all sorts pours into Britain, and, while I propose to discourse for a few pages, for an excellent beginner's guide on basic types of wines I refer readers to a companion volume, *The Pan Book of Wine*, wherein various authors write in terms the interested layman can understand. After that, a huge vinous literature is open to you.

A few years ago, when I started and edited for Harveys of Bristol an elegant quarterly I had titled *Vintage* (which, I will immodestly state, won a prize in the USA as the best journal in its field!) I arranged with that combination of wine expert, *bon vivant*, wit and sports-writer, Denzil Batchelor, that we should contribute companion pieces; he on being proud to be a wine snob and myself on the importance of not being one. I should add that Denzil said he would be quite happy if we swapped roles, for, of course, as a man who knows a lot about wine – and knows just how *much* he knows – he is not a wine snob at all. Which is the only reason why I mention the story: don't let a small knowledge of wine let you become a wine snob. Use, but don't unnecessarily air, such knowledge as you have. Don't condemn the person who prefers a *Sauternes* to a *Chablis*: some of the world's greatest wines are sweet, some 'dry' ones merely acid. Do not be condemnatory of the person who likes claret with fish or hock with steak: who made the 'rules' about what-goes-with-what anyway? Wine snobbery is one of the most common social faults. It was definitively summed up by a well-known cartoon of the late great James Thurber. The American host at a dinner party, referring to the wine, says: 'It is only a naïve domestic burgundy without any breeding, but I think you'll be amused at its presumption!'

The Great Beaujolais Myth

Of course, the aggressive *anti*-wine snob is as bad. You know, the man who insists that Portuguese claret is just as good as Château Lafite; who pours down chilled red burgundy and says it is all nonsense about having it room temperature. He's as bad as the one who fusses around carefully decanting a wine that hasn't been in bottle a month. Wine is for *drinking*. Red wines are better when not cold; white ones are better chilled (not iced to death), and the sweeter the wine the colder it should be. Ancient red wines do need careful handling. These are facts. Much wine lore is legend. Take Beaujolais. A great expert on wine once told me that to ensure getting a 100 per cent true Beaujolais into your cellar you would need to watch it without a pause from the day the grapes were picked. There is possibly more wine under the name Beaujolais drunk in England per month than the district, a large one, actually produces annually. Beaujolais is a light, red wine, normally drunk cooled in France. In Britain it has virtually become a name for simple 'red wine' and is treated as a burgundy, which it is not.

Many wines sold as Beaujolais are excellent full-bodied

table wines (their exact origin need not unduly trouble us) but don't get excited about them. Their prices vary extravagantly without much relation to quality. Pretentious restaurants will solemnly place an over-priced 'Beaujolais' in a wine-cradle and treat it with the reverence due to a venerable château-bottled *Bordeaux rouge*. There are some splendid wines such as Moulin-á-Vent which are technically Beaujolais, but they are invariably labelled under their prestige-carrying names.

Cautionary Tales

It is customary for the host at home to pour a little wine into his glass and taste it before pouring for guests. But he should have drawn the cork(s) previous to dinner, for it is correct that wine should 'breathe', and presumably he has tasted it then to see it is all right. To do so at table only proves it isn't poisoned! In restaurants, it may be judicious to taste a wine: it can be 'corked' or out of condition. In the case of rare wines, a good *sommelier* (wine waiter) will himself ensure that a wine is in perfect condition, but will also pour for the host's opinion. It is sometimes useful to decant a red wine that has been long in bottle, though careful pouring from a cradle should not disturb the sediment inevitably thrown by an aged claret.

In a restaurant one *may* not get the whole contents of a bottle when decanted: a good friend of mine in the catering business learned his considerable knowledge of wine through glasses he abstracted as assistant wine waiter (his boss got the other glass) in a leading London hotel! Don't begrudge this perk. However, it makes me writhe when I am offered a tasting of the *carafe* wines that are an excellent feature of many restaurants. If the establishment has no faith in its draught wines, it should not sell them.

Re restaurants, a slightly cautionary tale which was told before the war in a waiter's book of reminiscences. When he saw an obviously inexperienced young man, entertaining a girl to dinner, staring with some bewilderment at a huge wine list, he would at once recommend the cheapest wine on the page. The man would inevitably scorn this advice. He would then point at the very bottom to one of the costliest wines offered. This would also be rejected. He would then suggest a wine half-way down which would certainly be more expensive than the diner wanted but which would nearly always be accepted because the performance had gone on long enough and the young man was getting fidgety.

One of my most illuminating experiences in a restaurant was seeing a solitary diner complaining of the slowness of arrival of his wine. The waiter apologized, and I could, but the diner couldn't, see the ensuing pantomime. The waiter made urgent signs to the service hatch, a bottle sailed through the air, was dexterously caught by the waiter, who placed it in a wicker cradle, carried it to the table, ceremoniously uncorked it and poured out the ritual portion. The diner sipped it knowingly and nodded in acceptance.

As a youth, dining a contemporary in a great restaurant of the Champs-Elysées, I showed my worldly knowledge by studying the *carte des vins* and discussing in my then fluent but execrably accented French the merits of certain burgundies. My selection arrived and I was decidedly surprised by its taste. However, I nodded sagely and we drank it. I discovered it was a sparkling burgundy, of the existence of which I was then totally ignorant. 'I don't suppose you've ever had a sparkling Bourgogne before?' I said to my guest. He hadn't. I think it is a horrible wine, but I learned a good lesson: don't be too proud to admit ignorance.

Returning to the subject of wine snobbery: in his fascinating book *The Arches of the Years*, first published around 1930 and superior in my view to *San Michele*, Dr Halliday Sutherland tells of how he was in charge of wardroom wines in a big armed merchant vessel in World War I. Calling at Gibraltar, they decided to re-stock and invited samples from Saccone and Speed, the noted merchants. Dr Sutherland, steamed off the numbers by which the samples were identified, and reversed them so that the ordinary *vin de table* carried the number of a great vintage *Bordeaux* and so on. The committee of officers duly sat for a tasting. Solemnly they sampled number one, a fine vintage wine, but which was now identified as something quite ordinary. They pronounced this to be absolute muck, and worked their way through the list until coming to the simple *vin ordinaire* which, because they thought it was rare and old, they sipped with enthusiasm and declared it to be a memorable wine. They were not pleased with their medical officer when the humiliating deception came to light.

A Glass of Champagne

My father was once entertaining a notability who had moved into the district and decided to open some of his best champagne. He inquired first whether his guest liked champagne, and the answer was affirmative. He then asked what he thought of the particularly superb wine they were drinking. 'Oh, I don't care – as long as it bubbles', answered his distinguished visitor.

The British are enormous drinkers of champagne, and it is my opinion that a high percentage of it is drunk by people who don't really like it at all. A lot is consumed at weddings, and at parties where it is considered smart. Now, while quite a lot of people may like champagne in the evening, it is inconsiderately show-off not to provide spirits and other potables for those who do not like, or do not at that time of day care for, champagne.

Ideally, fine vintage champagne – or great non-vintage ones like Bollinger and Clicquot – should be as cold as they would be from a really deep cellar; lesser ones will benefit (at least, your palate will) if more deeply chilled. No ice *in* the wine, of course; not in any table wine when it is being served on its own.

I am glad to see that there has been a considerable revulsion against that English invention, the 'saucer' champagne glass, which was evolved so chorus girls of the nineties would not hiccup on too much effervescence in their bubbly. It takes years of time and hours and hours of labour to put the entirely natural bubbles into champagne, and the correct glass is a champagne flute, extremely elegant, which does not quickly dissipate the gas, now sold in Britain. Otherwise use an ordinary wine glass, preferably of tulip shape. Swizzle-sticks are another obnoxious medium for getting champagne to go flat. One reason why champagne is costly is the process of making it effervescent: if you don't like it that way, then try to obtain a still champagne: unfortunately, this *Champagne nature* is extremely hard to find today.

Whine Parties!

Wine is a great beverage, with food – other than champagne which, I opine, is best without food, and best of all quaffed from a silver tankard at noon! The habit of drinking table wines at other times, in the pub, at the cocktail hour at home, has much grown in Britain in recent years. Part of this is fiscal, doubtless, owing to the excessive taxation of spirits. Then there is the Wine Party, skilfully promoted in the interests of the Wine trade and the Cheese industry. Wine and cheese go splendidly together, but I don't think they

123

make much of a party by themselves – except perhaps for teenagers. It is waste to use fine vintages on such an occasion, and most folk soon tire of imbibing lesser wines on their own. If economy rules the entertainment, jolly up ordinary wine by turning it into some sort of Punch, and, again, do try to have some alternative drinks even if you hoard them for special friends who you know only like gin or whisky: you don't want your Wine Party to become a Whine Party!

One thing you won't find in this book is a vintage chart. It has no place, to start with, and also, while popular, these charts can be infernally misleading. We all know some years produce better wines than others, but it's got so that people think any wine of a much publicized 'good' year must be splendid, regardless of type, shipper or other consideration. In extreme cases, the bottle may not even contain wine of the stated year. Better a wine with no year on it from a trusted shipper than a portentous 'vintage' and no further guarantee. And in anything but the rare years of total vinous disaster, there will be some excellent wines: weather – the main arbiter of grape harvest quality – is a capricious beast, and may change within a few miles.

In the following recipes, where CLARET is mentioned, any sound inexpensive *Bordeaux Rouge* or equivalent will suffice; BURGUNDY, a *Macon rouge*, *Côtes du Rhone*, Australian, or similar styles from Spain, Italy, Portugal, Cyprus, or elsewhere; for HOCK, a simple *Liebfraumilch*, or a *Riesling* from South Africa, Jugoslavia, etc.; for CHABLIS any very dry white wine; for SAUTERNES, any sweet white one. Various comparatively inexpensive CHAMPAGNES are available, suitable for mixed Cups, but for a Champagne Cocktail use a well-known non-vintage brand (don't waste vintage by adulteration). 'Champagne-type' wines – champagne is now a protected name and may be applied only to the genuine French article – are adequate for some mixtures but tend to lack flavour. In most punches you can afford to use quite cheap wines, as mollifying ingredients will tone down any sharp edges.

André Simon says only 2 per cent of the world's annual wine production are 'quality wines'. The remaining odd 3,500 million gallons we can, therefore, reasonably use for mixed drinks!

> 'Diogenes was asked what wine he liked best; and he answered as I would have done when he said, "Somebody else's".'
>
> *Montaigne*

WAYS WITH WINE

1. Bishop

Tablespoon Powdered Sugar
2 dashes Lemon Juice
Juice of ½ an orange
Wine-glass of Soda-Water

Dissolve these together in a tall glass, half fill with ice, and top with Burgundy. Stir well and top with a sprinkling of Jamaica Rum. Add a little Seasonable Fruit. Serve with straws.

(You can look up 'Bishop' in six books and get six very different answers. This is an old American recipe. See also 'English Bishop'; recipes after Chapter 13.)

2. Burgundy Mull

1 bottle Red Burgundy
1 wine-glass Dry Sherry
2 oz. Brandy
Small bottle Blackcurrant Cordial
1 quart water
3 Lemons, Sugar, Ginger, Cloves

Slice Lemons small and place in saucepan. Add cupful Sugar and teaspoon Ginger. Mix well and add remainder ingredients. Heat but do not boil. Add Cloves; strain, and serve hot in teacups.

3. Champagne A L'Orange

A mixture of between half-and-half well-chilled Champagne and Fresh Orange Juice, with or without $\frac{1}{2}$ oz. Cognac. (In London called a 'Bucks' Fizz'.)

4. Champagne Cocktail

1 lump of Sugar in bottom of large wine-glass, on which has been shaken three dashes of Angostura; add $\frac{1}{2}$ oz. Cognac, and top with very cold Champagne. Serve with round of Orange on top.

(Individual opinions vary on this drink, of which the prestige may largely be due to its cost.)

5. Champagne Punch

2 bottles non-vintage Dry Champagne
4 oz. Brandy
3 oz. Cointreau

3 oz. Maraschino
Siphon Soda-Water

Mix ingredients (except Champagne and Soda) and chill.
Add the Iced Champagne and Chilled Soda-Water just
before serving and decorate bowl with Fruit. Try to keep as
cool as possible without undue ice dilution.

6. Claret Cup

1 Lemon
1 Orange
6 slices fresh Pineapple
1½ oz. each—
    Brandy
    Cointreau
    Sugar Syrup
Tablespoon Lemon Juice

Slice Orange and Lemon and over them in very large glass
jug pour the other ingredients with large ice lumps. Add 1
bottle Light Red Wine, siphon Soda-Water; stir, decorate
with Fruit.

7. Chicago

1 oz. Cognac
Teaspoon Cointreau
2 dashes Angostura

Stir and strain into wine goblet of which the lip has been
dipped in iced water and then frosted with Powdered Sugar.
Fill with chilled non-vintage Champagne.

8. Forte's Fizz

1 oz. Vodka
1 oz. Cassis

Top with very cold Dry Champagne. No ice in the drink.
Stir well. Decorate with round of Lemon.

J.D. / Jules Bar, London

9. Kir

4 oz. chilled Dry White Burgundy; teaspoon Cassis. Ice at
own discretion.

French Bartenders' Assn

10. Mulled Red Wine

2 bottles ordinary Red Wine
⅓ bottle inexpensive Port
¼ bottle Brandy
A lemon stuffed with cloves
Peel of 2 Lemons
Teaspoon Nutmeg
3 Cinnamon sticks

Bring to near boiling very slowly, stirring the while and
adding Brown Sugar to taste. Serve in mugs.

11. Red Wine Punch

2 bottles robust Red Wine
1 bottle Port
½ bottle Cherry Brandy
Juice of 6 Oranges and 4 Lemons
¼ lb. Powdered Sugar

Mix chilled ingredients in large bowl. Add siphon Soda-Water. Place large lumps of ice in bowl and float on surface rounds of Fresh Fruit.

12. '75
2 oz. Dry Gin
Juice of 1 Lemon
Teaspoon Powdered Sugar
2 dashes Angostura

Shake, strain into tall stemmed glass. Top with chilled non-vintage Champagne.

13. White Wine Punch
⅓ pint Sugar Syrup
¾ pint Lemon Juice
½ bottle Brandy
bottle of Dry Sherry
3 bottles Dry White Wine
Two large cups Strong Tea

Mix in large punch-bowl and refrigerate. Before serving add siphon Soda-Water and decorate with rounds of Cucumber.

14. Wine Sangaree
Heaped teaspoon of Powdered Sugar in a tall glass. Dissolve in a little of your preferred Wine, add 2 ice cubes and top with same, preferably Dry, White, Wine. Stir once or twice.

CHAPTER 13

Fortified Wines – Sherry, Port, Madeira

AS OPPOSED to the last chapter, we can now, possibly to the relief of the reader, return from opinion to fact, since it is quite possible to give an outline of the wines in question. These are classified as 'fortified' because at some stage in their production spirit is added.

SHERRY has long been a favourite wine in Britain, and was certainly blood-brother to the Sack of which Falstaff was fond. Demand in the wine has changed; sweeter varieties were once 'smart', while it is drier ones (or at least with Dry in their titles) that are mostly now popular. In Victorian times, men sometimes took sherry with bitters, and certain fine mixed drinks can be made from sherry, particularly for summer use.

There are two basic types of sherry – *Fino*, pale and dry; *Oloroso*, darker and sweeter. *Amontillado*, perhaps the most popular type in Britain, is a slightly stronger and less dry edition of *fino*. *Manzanilla* is a *fino* that has been stored at Sanlucar, on the coast, where it acquires from the salt air of the Atlantic that peculiar character which makes it the favourite of lovers of extra-dry sherries. Brown sherry is darkened and sweetened (mainly) *Oloroso*. *Oloroso* is the type to which many of the famous cream sherries belong. (Note: Bristol Milk has existed for six hundred years; that name is not protected. There are many Bristol Milks. By chance, Bristol Cream, allegedly named by a lady visiting their cellars – was registered by Harveys and belongs solely to them. Incidentally the war-established Food Ministry threatened them with prosecution for implying the use of cream when this dairy product was prohibited!) There are numerous other excellent cream sherries bearing famous names in sherry, the trade in which has long been dominated by English family firms – Mackenzie, Byass, Williams & Humbert and so on. Many of them – though no longer Harveys – are still under family control.

A characteristic of sherry production is the Solera system, which, explained briefly, means that as wines well rested in cask are drawn off, the butts are topped up from one containing a slightly younger wine, which in turn are filled with wines younger still. The process is analagous to that carried out at Cognac with brandy.

Sherries in commerce are all blended, to maintain consistent brand character. The whole trade centres on Jerez de la Frontera, where are the biggest Bodegas – giant, aboveground 'cellars' – which strike cool on the hottest day, and the temperature in this part of Andalusia reaches Sahara levels in high summer, which is not the time to visit the charming town, said to have the highest per capita income in Spain. It is well worth visiting at other times, particularly if you have an introduction in the trade.

As the result of a Court ruling, in Britain the word Sherry, on its own, may only be used to describe a Spanish wine, and while undoubtedly the finest sherries come from Spain, there are ones possibly of even better *value* from South Africa whose wine industry is by no means new though now highly modernized technically. Australia is a big sherry producer; but it is, as with her excellent table wines (excluding her 'champagne'), difficult for her to send wines half-way round the world to compete with nearer producers. A pity, for Australian wine products are good, and we only see a few burgundies in regular retail in Britain. Cyprus produces a tolerable sherry.

Importance of Port

PORT is a highly protected name, and in Britain only wine entirely produced in Portugal according to Portuguese law may use this title; any imitations must carry such words as 'type' or 'style'. Portwine is virtually an English invention, for the beautiful heavy wine of that name has little attraction elsewhere. (If you have drunk, as an aperitif, the 'porto' of France, you will know it bears little relation to port). As a result, the trade is dominated, as with sherry, by British names. Britain's wine trade with Portugal antedates the coming of port as we know it (and the import of Portuguese table wines has lately greatly increased; witness the spectacular success of Mateus Rosé).

Vintage port is a thing apart; one of the great drinks of the world. And it has absolutely no connexion with mixed drinks of any kind. But portwine has, both historically and in our time. By the way, we may as well dispose of the old 'four (or more) bottle man' of legend in connexion with port. Our forefathers who indulged till they fell under the table were not drinking the strongly fortified port we know, but virtually a table wine.

All ports (excluding Vintage) are blended, so that your preferred brand will always taste the same. They are in the trade divided into 'Ruby' which is bottled comparatively young and will slowly improve in bottle, and 'Tawny' which is much longer matured in wood and does not improve in bottle. A 'vintage-style' port of exceptional merit is Taylor's.

White port, a true portwine made from white grapes, is

decidedly drier than red ports. At one time little esteemed, perhaps on the back of the vogue for pale drinks this excellent wine is achieving some popularity as an aperitif: it will stand chilling, having decided character, and bolder experimenters in the mixed drink field may substitute it for other styles when making up Cups.

Have A Madeira Me Dear

MADEIRA wine has been known in Britain for centuries, though doubt is cast on whether it was actually a butt of madeira (malmsey) in which the ill-fated Duke of Clarence was drowned. 'Malmsey' is the traditional English name for *Bual*, a sweet madeira; the other two being *Verdelho* (medium-sweet) and *Sercial* (dry). Madeira is made in a distinctive way on the island that gives it its name. The new wine is fortified with highly rectified local molasses spirit and rested in heated stores (hence it is sometimes referred to as being a 'cooked' wine), is further fortified and then goes into casks for long maturing. This ageing process being essential to madeira, barrels of it were once used as ship's ballast, which gave rise to the notion that a round-world sea voyage improved the wine. This is unlikely, but madeira enjoys greater longevity than any other wine. It has never caught on in modern times like sherry or port, but has a devoted following. The wheel of fashion in drinking is unpredictable: a century ago no one would have prophesied that Scotch would sweep the world, that London's gin would receive the accolade of international fame . . . so who can say that in another century madeira may not be known to all?

Other fortified wines include *Marsala*, the Italian equivalent (English invented) of madeira; and *Malaga*, a blend of sweet Spanish wines. Fortified wines may be kept, after opening, in corked bottles or in decanters, and, unlike table wines, will remain in good condition for some time, though by no means indefinitely.

> 'I don't care where the water goes if it doesn't get into the wine.'
>
> *G. K. Chesterton*

MIXED DRINKS WITH FORTIFIED WINES

1. Adonis

2 oz. Dry Sherry
1 oz. Sweet Vermouth
Dash of Angostura

Stir, strain into cocktail-glass. (Do not over-ice).

2. Bombay Sherry Punch

1 bottle Sherry
1 bottle Brandy
Tablespoon Maraschino and Cointreau
2 bottles Fizzy Dry White Wine (something less than Champagne will suffice)
Siphon Soda-Water

Mix with large ice lumps (except wine) in large bowl.
Decorate with Fruit in season. Add Fizzy Wine at last moment.

3. Boston

1 oz. Dry Madeira
1 oz. American Whiskey

Level teaspoon Powdered Sugar
1 Egg Yolk

Shake vigorously, strain into goblet.
Top with Grated Nutmeg.

4. Devil's Cocktail

½ Port
½ Dry Vermouth
2 dashes Lemon Juice

Shake, strain into cocktail-glass.
Savoy

5. English Bishop

Stick 12 Cloves in an Orange; bake in moderate oven until well browned. Cut into quarters and place in suitable bowl. Pour on top a bottle of heated Port. Add Sugar to required sweetness while returning mixture to stove and continuing to heat gently, covered, for half an hour.

All sorts of Spices, plus Rum and Brandy, may be added according to individual inclination and enterprise (See 'Bishop'; recipes after Chapter 12.)

6. Glogg

Bottle of Medium Sherry
Bottle of Red Wine
3 oz. Powdered Sugar
8 dashes Angostura
½ bottle of Brandy

Heat without boiling. In warmed small mugs put a couple of Raisins and an Unsalted Almond. Pour mixture on top.

(There are many variations on this Scandinavian winter warmer.)

7. Jerez Cocktail

2 oz. Dry Sherry
dash of Orange Bitters
dash of Peach Bitters

Stir well and strain into cocktail-glass.

8. Marco Polo

Hot Punch for about 30 persons:
2 bottles Medium Madeira
½ lb. Sugar
10 oz. Otard Cognac
10 sticks Cinnamon
10 slices Lemon

Stick each slice of Lemon liberally with Cloves. Heat all ingredients slowly, stirring constantly, until near boiling. Serve very warm in teacups.
    London Hilton

9. Port Cocktail

2 oz. Port Wine
dash Cognac

Stir, strain. Squeeze Orange peel on top.

10. Portwine Flip

1 substantial glass of Port
1 teaspoon Powdered Sugar
1 Egg Yolk

Shake well and strain into small tumbler. Sprinkle on a little Cinnamon.

11. Savoy Springbok

⅓ Sherry
⅓ Lillet
⅓ Van der Hum
2 dashes Orange Bitters

Stir, strain into cocktail-glass.

12. Sherry Cobbler

Put 3 oz. Medium Sherry in tall glass and mix with teaspoon
Powdered Sugar. Add plenty of cracked ice, top with Soda-
Water, add dash of Grenadine, stir.

Serve with rounds of Seasonable Fruit.

13. Sherry Cocktail

2 oz. Sherry
4 dashes Orange Bitters
3 dashes Dry Vermouth

Stir well, and strain into cocktail-glass.

14. Sherry Flip

2 oz. Dry Sherry
1 Egg
Teaspoon Powdered Sugar
2 dashes Angostura

Shake briskly, strain into stemmed glass; top with Grated
Nutmeg.

15. Sloppy Joe

1 oz. Port
1 oz. Brandy
2 oz. Pineapple Juice
2 dashes Cointreau

Shake, strain into small wine-glass.

16. Sunrise

⅔ substantial wine-glass Port
⅓ wine-glass Brandy
Several drops of Angostura
1 oz. Vanilla Syrup

Shake well, strain into chilled tumbler and garnish with Lemon rind.

17. Syllabub

per serving—
2 oz. Sweet Sherry
1 oz. double Cream
1 oz. Milk
Teaspoon Powdered Sugar

Beat together, testing for sweetness, and serve with teaspoons in shallow glasses.

(Not so much a drink, more a form of dessert.)

CHAPTER 14

Liqueurs – The Cocktail's Friends

WHEN someone says 'Will you have a liqueur'?, it may refer to a *liqueur* brandy or a dessert sherry (but not to port-wine – port is *Port*); yet the chances are high that the reference is to one or a selection of the vast number of diverse sweet (plus a few dry) liqueurs.

Apart from their individual merits on their own, most of the best known liqueurs are essential ingredients of some Cocktails, and the best way for me to deal with them is to list alphabetically the most famous types and brands (many are unique, with imitations of varying efficacy) together with a very brief description for your guidance, adding titbits of prejudice and information. There are hundreds of regional liqueurs, and variations of types, so I only give those in reasonably normal commerce and use in Britain: this book is not intended as a guide for hedonistic seekers of the exotic. (Proprietary brands are in small capitals):

Advocaat – best made by the Dutch; composed of egg-yolks and sugar, dissolved in brandy (WARNINK, FOCKINK, etc).

Anis, Anisette, Anice – in sundry forms, strongly aniseed-flavoured liqueurs.

APRY, Abricotine – fine apricot brandy.

BENEDICTINE – I don't hesitate to name this my number one favourite. Based on finest cognac, and, though widely copied, no one has broken the secret which dates from its monkish discovery in 1510. The famous DOM initials on the bottle do not, as is sometimes thought, stand for Dominican Order of Monks (nor for Dirty Old Man!) but for *Deo Optimo Maximo* ('To God, most Good, most Great'). 'Bene' is sometimes taken mixed half-and-half with cognac. If you prefer it this way, better to buy it in its proprietary 'B and B' form; they know how to blend it in Fécamp.

CHARTREUSE – it is the green that is very strong; the yellow is milder. This superb liqueur dates from 1676 and is still under French monastic charge, but the Carthusian monks suffered persecution and in 1903 were expelled, taking their secret to Spain where the nectar is still produced as well as in France.

Cherry brandy – self-descriptive; CHERRY HEERING, CHERRY ROCHER, etc. Well I remember trying as a boy to get a sherry in Paris: they always brought me cherry brandy!

COINTREAU – one of the relatively few absolutely world-famous liqueurs, a superb quality cognac-based liqueur of the orange Curaçao type; invaluable to Cocktail-makers.

Crème de Càcao – cocoa-flavoured and syrupy. There are *crème* liqueurs of infinite variety – amongst others: banana, nut, coffee, raspberry, strawberry, violets, roses; even tea. '*Crème*' indicates very sweet rich liqueurs; as such they can have considerable use as flavoured substitutes for sugar in cocktails. However,

Crème de Menthe (CUSENIER, etc.), deserves separate mention. Less sweet and coming in green or white, the latter being the drier. Numerous well-known continental brands are made with great care from various mints, not only peppermint.

Curaçao – generic term for an originally white rum-based cordial flavoured with the rind of a special local orange grown on the Dutch West Indies island of the same name.

Liqueurs of this style are widely produced with brandy or neutral spirit bases.

DRAMBUIE – the fantastically successful Scottish liqueur taking its name from 'an dram buidheach' (the drink that satisfies). Its origins have legendary connexions with Bonnie Prince Charlie, who is said to have confided the recipe to one of the Mackinnons in 1745, for saving his life: Mackinnon *and* Flora MacDonald! The family started marketing the liqueur at the end of the last century and still guard its secrets with much mystery. It is flavoured with heather-honey and other herbs, and is based only on the finest Scotch whisky.

GALLIANO – this distinctive yellow Italian liqueur has come rapidly up the charts in the USA, has been in at least one prize-winning Cocktail in Europe, and can be expected to get more widely known in Britain.

Goldwasser (Eau d'Or), 'Golden Water', is particularly associated with ancient Danzig and is a liqueur of immense antiquity. Not too sweet, with a lemon-style flavour, some people like it if only because when you shake the bottle thousands of minute specks of real gold float in the white spirit. (I've only put this one in for aesthetic reasons; the gold wouldn't show in a Cocktail).

GRAND MARNIER – the great golden orange-flavoured liqueur of France, of no great antiquity, but which some connoisseurs prefer to all others. Based on the finest fine champagne cognac.

IRISH MIST: Ireland's fine riposte to Drambuie.

KAHLUA – the Mexican coffee-flavoured liqueur which, in my opinion, deserves wider distribution in Britain. It can be drunk instead of having coffee and a separate liqueur: it really combines the two.

Kümmel – this has been made for a very long time in various continental cities, notably in Riga and in Germany; today perhaps the Dutch are making the best. There are numerous brands (one may perhaps single out BOLS) that are excellent; they vary in sweetness but are always white. The aniseed, caraway, cumin content gives it widely vaunted digestive powers. Mixed half-and-half with 'High & Dry' gin, to reduce the sweetness, it is known within my company as 'Gümmel' (patent pending!).

Lemon gin: as with orange gin and sloe gin, see Notes on GIN.

Maraschino – a very sweet cordial that has many Cocktail uses. Though made elsewhere, it is associated with the wild cherries of the Dalmatian coast. Much more used in mixed drinks than drunk on its own.

Fior D'Alpi (also Eidelweiss and Millefiori) – Gimmick Italian liqueurs with a miniature tree in the bottle: the trick is to get the sugar to crystallize on the branches, which will happen if you don't let it get too warm. The tree adds nothing to otherwise light, sugary, quite attractive liqueurs of various makes and no particular distinction: Christmas-time fun, perhaps.

Prunella – plum-flavoured brandy.

STREGA – sweet, aromatic citrus-based liquor, very popular in Italy, of which several other forms exist. The word means 'witch'.

TIA MARIA – Jamaica's very own liqueur, coffee-flavoured on a fine light Rum base; it has greatly grown in popularity in Britain since the war.

TRAPPISTINE – seems to have an affinity with Benedictine but is based on armagnac.

VAN DER HUM – the rough translation is said to be 'What's-his-name'. This popular and distinctive South African liqueur is based on tangerines and brandy with other herbal ingredients.

VIEILLE CURE – though the pronunciation of the final word would be right, and the description good enough, it would be wrong to translate this as 'the ancient cure'. Actually it means 'the old rectory', an allusion to its origins in an Abbey at Bordeaux. A great liqueur, better known in France than Britain.

Nearly all the liqueurs, generic or proprietary, mentioned in this far from exhaustive list will be found in various recipes after other chapters. However, there are a few modern Cocktails that have come to my notice which appear to be specific inventions connected with certain liqueurs. It may seem invidious to select these for special mention; however, enterprise merits some reward. There is no reason why a traditional potable should not become the basis of a new drink, provided it be sensible and not abrasive to a fine liquor.

'A soft drink turneth away company.'
Oliver Herford

DRINKS WHERE LIQUEURS STAND OUT

1. Between the Sheets

⅓ Cointreau
⅓ Cognac
⅓ light Rum
Dash of Lemon Juice

Shake, strain into cocktail-glass.

2. Black Russian

½ Kahlua
½ Vodka

Serve 'on the rocks'.
California Bartenders' Guild

3. Bull Frog

1½ oz. Apricot Brandy
Juice of 1 Lemon

Shake briskly, strain into cocktail-glass.

4. Charlie Chaplin

1½ oz. Sloe Gin
2 teaspoons unsweetened Lime Juice
½ oz. Apricot Brandy

Shake, strain into cocktail-glass.

5. Cointreau Rocks

In small tumbler pour 3 oz. Cointreau over 3 ice cubes.
Add 3 dashes Angostura. Stir.
(Slice of Lemon optional).

6. Copa de Oro

1 oz. Grand Marnier
1 oz. Tequila Sauza
Teaspoon Sugar
1 Egg

Shake with cracked ice and serve in wine-glass, its top
covered by a round of Orange with straws through it.

CHAPTER 15

Beer, Cider – and a Digression on Pubs

IF YOU want to know how beer is made, the best step is to get leave to look round a brewery: a very interesting experience. Most people are quite content simply to drink the stuff.

Being again faced here with the immensity of the subject, for British beers alone are complex enough, let alone those of a hundred other countries, I withdraw temporarily from the descriptive world and put forward a few thoughts on Pubs; for beer and pubs are inseparable. Anyway, a book without digressions is a dull one!

Certain trends in the trade have made a radical change in British beer which is not apparent to the young but very much so to anyone who has been enjoying Pubs for thirty years. True old-fashioned draught bitter beer, needing the tender and expert care of that dying race – the dedicated publican and/or his cellarman – is under conditions of modern rationalized commerce giving way to pressurized bitter, forced from the cellar by compressed air. Keg bitters, which require no more attention than to link them to a tap, ring a further death-knell for the old beer-engine and its decorative handles. Doubtless a great boon to all concerned.

I have seen coffee machines hiss where formerly were snug or parlour, and it is common for elaborate snacks and infra-red grilled steaks to be eaten at counters where once the honest toiler leaned between pulls at his pint of ale. The Classless Society is reflected in the one-bar tavern, more like a hotel

7. Jamaican Wonder

½ oz. Tia Maria
1 oz. Lemon Hart Rum
1 oz. Unsweetened Lime Juice
Dash of Angostura

Place in tall glass and fill with chilled Bitter Lemon.

8. Hell

1 oz. Crème de Menthe
1 oz. Brandy

Shake, strain into cocktail-glass.
Top with Cayenne Pepper.

9. Round the World

1½ oz. Green Crème de Menthe
2½ oz. Fresh Pineapple Juice
1 oz. Dry Gin

Shake, strain into large cocktail-glass. Garnish, if practicable, with piece of Pineapple on stick.

10. Snowball

Ice cube in tall glass. Generous measure of Advocaat; top with Fizzy Lemonade; decorate with slice of Lemon.

lounge than the variegated compartments of the traditional British pub. Or, elsewhere, rather 'camp' pseudo-Victorian (the latest craze is Edwardian) decors replace the genuine. Having allowed the old nostalgia to have its say, let us remember it is pointless to repine or to be a Square drinker in a Round public house. Let us look upon the credit side.

The average drinker seems to like his antiseptic beers, pasteurized, clarified, ever-ready: and there *are* many other beers still around. The new pubs are cleaner, if not necessarily friendlier, than many they replaced. Piped music, juke boxes, one-armed bandits, bands and pop groups may bring in more new customers than they drive out old. It is necessary to compete with magnificently equipped industrial Clubs. Yet I hope the brewers will finally leave standing – plus new mod cons by all means – not just Historic Inns but some typical, ordinary, urban pubs.

What Do You Think?

The gradual passing of Mine Host is also, perhaps, an inevitable erosion of the old by the new. I know it is easy to romanticize the jolly Victorian publican with fat face and heavy gold Albert across his corpulence. That he was quite often a grasping ruffian beneath the veneer, who bullied his staff and watered his ale, is not to be denied. Yet we have all, who are over forty, known Landlords – tenants of a brewer maybe – independent, proud of 'their' houses, characters. We probably still know some, but certainly fewer. Is this just another trend of inevitable modernization of what was once a much friendlier, cosier, more personal business? It has brought increased efficiency: has it brought anything else? What do *you* think?

Things it has brought are more continental beers, fresh British ones, new packagings, cans, and big party packs which, incidentally, are splendid foundations for beer-based Punches.

The best beer for most beer-based drinks is mild ALE or Burton (draught) when you can get it; in the South this type seems to have lost favour. BITTER beer may be used in place of ale but the sharpness of this is not suitable to some mixed drinks. STOUT has a special place, and a Black Velvet made with draught Guinness (rather than bottled) is a great restorative (some authors might have included it under pick-me-ups; yet I think it is a splendid drink when you are feeling perfectly well but don't mind feeling better: it is my personal preference as an accompaniment to oysters). LAGER has little place in mixed drinks. The costlier imported ones are often served excessively chilled – one loses some flavour thereby. While now widely applied to a type of light pale beer, the word Lager was originally a dark or pale beer long stored in a cellar (*lager*). IPA (India Pale Ale) originated as an export to India. Fine Pale Ales (such as Whitbread's Light) are being promoted as socially acceptable drinks for home entertainment, and quite rightly, where they were once confined mainly to the Pub. One can see a general rise in the status of beer.

CIDER is a drink scarcely less ancient than beer. Broadly, it is fermented apple juice, clarified and filtered. It used to be said that a dead horse was a good way to get the fermentation going: this is certainly not true today! Ranging from very sweet to very dry, strong to mild; coming still, carbonated or naturally effervescent through a 'champagne' process, cider makes a particularly splendid and inexpensive base for various exhilarating Cups and the like – good party stuff. It mixes well with most spirits, but any such combination, however blandseeming, should be treated circumspectly as it may contain a hidden left-hook to the stomach.

PERRY is, effectively, cider made from pears.

Where in recipes I do not specify an effervescent (or
'champagne') cider, draught is preferable, though not
essential.

> 'Come landlord fill a flowing bowl
> So that it doth run over;
> Tonight we will all merry be—
> Tomorrow we'll get sober.'
>
> *John Fletcher*

BEER AND CIDER DRINKS

1. Ale Flip

Teaspoon Powdered Sugar
1 Egg
Small wine-glass strong IPA

Shake, strain into goblet. Top with Grated Nutmeg.

2. Ale Flip (Hot)

Grate peel of a Lemon and mix with pint of Strong Ale.
Heat without boiling. Beat in a mixture of 4 Eggs, 2 oz.
Demerara, level teaspoon Nutmeg, 3 oz. Brandy.

Serve in mugs.

149

3. Apple Cocktail

⅓ Sweet Cider
⅙ Dry Gin
⅙ Brandy
⅓ Apple Brandy (Calvados)

Shake very cold, strain into large cocktail-glass.

4. Beer Sangaree

Dissolve a teaspoon of Sugar in a little water at the bottom of a long glass. Top with the Chilled Beer of your choice (a Dark Strong Ale is best) and top with Grated Nutmeg. No ice in drink itself.

5. Booth's 'With It' Punch – for about 14 persons

Quart of Medium-Sweet Cider
½ bottle 'Booth's' Gin
½ bottle Advocaat
Juice of 4 Lemons
Split-size bottle Soda-Water

Mix thoroughly in large bowl or jug with plenty of ice, adding Soda at last moment. Decorate with rounds of Lemon. Serve in wine-glasses.

6. Black Velvet

½ Guinness
½ Champagne (iced)

Use tankard, preferably silver. No ice in drink.

7. Cider Cup

1 flagon Dry Cider
½ pint Orange Squash or Fresh Juice
Juice of 1 Lemon
6 tablespoons Cointreau

Thoroughly chill Cider. Mix it with ingredients, adding siphon of Soda-Water, slices of Orange and Lemon, Cocktail Cherries, and ice at last moment.

Serve in wine-glasses.

8. Devonia Cocktail

Pour into the shaker 8 oz. Sparkling Cider and 4 oz. Gin. Add some ice and a few drops of Orange Bitters. Shake lightly and serve.

Savoy

9. Guinness Cooler

⅔ liqueur glass Cointreau
⅔ liqueur glass Crème de Càcao
1 liqueur glass Dubonnet

Pour over ice in large goblet. Fill with Guinness and decorate with spiral of Apple peel.

Mr Eddie Clarke

10. Mulled Spiced Ale

Dissolve teaspoon of Powdered Sugar in metal ½ pint tankard, adding pinch of Powdered Cinnamon. Top with Strong Dark Beer of your choice and heat by inserting a white-hot poker.

(In these days of all gas/electric homes you may have to heat the beer by other means, but it isn't half as much fun.)

11. Turkish Blood

In a pint tankard mix—
half-and-half Burton XXX Ale (or Russian Stout) and Red Burgundy.
    Do not ice.

CHAPTER 16

Softly, Softly – Abstainer's Selection

I DO NOT think I have ever taken a completely non-alcoholic 'Cocktail' – though I have been to parties where the Cocktail *appeared* non-alcoholic! However, we sociable drinkers are broad-minded: why should not those who for one reason or another – good or bad – do not touch alcohol in even the mildest form be deprived of recipes for mixed drinks ? Here are a few, culled in my researches, and originally rejected as lacking zest. I am sure some of them are excellent, and your TT friends might be flattered to be offered one at a party, for many of them look like *Cocktails*: I know that vegetarians eat nut *cutlets* and vegetable *escalopes*.

SHLOER, the pure English apple juice drink, can produce interesting variations on our sober theme. The makers suggest: a pint tankard three-quarters filled with very cold shloer, and then add juice of an orange, slices of apple, cucumber, mint, Cocktail cherries and ice. Or, to a small glass of chilled shloer add a few drops of unflavoured food-colouring, turning something non-alcoholic into a wicked-seeming drink. A considerable range of drinks may be produced from this pleasant fruit juice.

'He drank like a fish, if drinking nothing but water could be so described.'

A. E. Housman

NON-ALCOHOLIC MIXES AND 'MOCKTAILS'

1. Cardinal Punch

In suitable container over lump of ice, pour 2 pints Cranberry Juice, 1 pint Fresh Orange Juice, Juice of 2 Lemons, 4 bottles chilled Canada Dry Ginger Ale.

2. Limey

1 oz. Rose's Lime Juice
½ oz. Fresh Lemon Juice
Teaspoon Egg White

Shake, strain into cocktail-glass.

3. Parson's Particular

2 oz. Fresh Orange Juice
1 oz. Lemon Juice
Yolk of an Egg
4 dashes Grenadine

Shake briskly, strain into large cocktail-glass.

4. Pussyfoot

⅓ Lemon Juice
⅓ Orange Juice
⅓ Unsweetened Lime Juice
Dash of Grenadine or half-teaspoon Powdered Sugar
Yolk of one Egg

Shake well and strain into wine-glass.
Top with Soda-Water. Serve with Cocktail Cherry on stick.

5. Temperance Mocktail

3 oz. Lemon Juice
1 oz. Sugar Syrup (or Grenadine)
Yolk of an Egg

Shake briskly, strain into large cocktail-glass.

CHAPTER 17

Hair of the Dog

IT IS only the very wise who have never suffered, even mildly, from that matutinal malaise or alcoholic remorse to which the ugly and descriptive word Hangover applies. While it is a fallacy to believe that 'mixing drinks', drinking spirits and wine and beer – and all that jazz – in the same evening, induces extra intoxication, injudicious mixing *may* unnecessarily upset the stomach. The degree of intoxication rests on the amount of alcohol consumed, plus, possibly, certain psychological factors though these do not affect a person's inebriation in the clinical sense.

Before festive evenings, certain precautions may be taken by the compulsively convivial. Creamy milk or olive oil – or a preliminary snack of the sardines on buttered toast variety – will provide some protection against too quick effects from drinks taken on an empty stomach. Don't miss dinner on any account. Before going to bed, *if* one then remembers to, is the time to take one's Seltzer (Alka- or Bromo-), to drink a lot of water, or lime-juice and water, or a Pinta Milka.

Inexorably comes the morning, grey and acid, and there is really not a great deal one can do. It is said that the ancient Romans, if bitten by a dog, to ward off ill-effects would drink a potion containing burnt hair from that canine. Hence the true hair-of-the-dog treatment, by which, if one has been over-indulgent with, say, the brandy, one should pour down some more of the same spirit at the earliest permissible hour. This is, of course, another fallacy. To add alcohol to a body already suffering from an excess of alcohol cannot do any good, medically speaking. Yet, by inducing a feeling of well-being, illusory and temporary relief may indeed be found.

Many people have their own specifics against the dreaded Hangover. A universally esteemed 'cure' is a pint of champagne: an esoteric use of 'Champers' involves sprinkling cayenne pepper on a glass of it. This produces an euphoria which may pass for health; and a desire for a further bottle. By that time one is completely cured, but, unfortunately, all set thoroughly to celebrate one's reunion with the living and one is thus on the road to self-perpetuating or chronic Hangover.

Some swear by the recuperative powers of Fernet-Branca. For myself, I find a little bottle of Underberg poured down the throat will work wonders within twenty minutes. I have also tried most of the following recipes with some degree of, at least ephemeral, success:

1. 'Hair Of The Dog' Cocktail

1 oz. Scotch
1½ oz. Heavy Cream
½ oz. Honey

Shake vigorously (if you can stand the noise) with shaved ice and strain into cocktail glass.

2. 'Prairie Oyster'

Mix, without ice, 1 oz. Cognac; teaspoonful wine vinegar; teaspoonful Worcester Sauce; dash of Red Pepper. Pour over the Yolk of an Egg and drink without breaking the egg. (There are several versions of the drink.)

3. 'Bullshot'

A can of Campbell's Condensed Consommé
2 oz. Vodka, or Very Dry Gin
Teaspoonful Worcester Sauce
Juice of half a Lemon
Dash of Red Pepper

Mix vigorously with plenty of ice and strain into big tumbler. (This can take the place of breakfast the morning after.)

4. 'Bloody Mary'

1 oz Vodka
A bottle, or small can, of Iced Tomato Juice
Dash of Celery Salt
Dash of Red Pepper
Teaspoonful Worcester Sauce

Stir together in tall glass, with a little cracked ice.

This is capable of personal variations. I make mine, called a 'Red Lion', with 'High and Dry' Gin, in order to maintain my ration of salubrious oil of juniper. It can also be made with Tequila, in which case the drink is known as 'Sangre'.

5. 'Corpse Reviver'

⅓ Brandy
⅓ Fernet Branca
⅓ White Crème de Menthe

Shake with ice and strain into cocktail-glass.
Savoy Hotel

6. 'Heart-Starter'

Good measure Dry Gin in tumbler of iced water.
Add heaped teaspoon Andrews Liver Salts.
Toss down quickly; and wait.

7. 'Pick-me-up' Cocktail

1 teaspoonful sugar
Dash of Angostura Bitters
1½ oz. Cognac
½ pint Fresh Milk
   Shake well with ice and strain into tall glass; top with
squirt of Soda-Water.
   UKBG

The only actual cure for the Screaming-Meemies is rest,
light diet, and lots of pure water. Yet I know of at least one
man who believes in an enormous breakfast on the basis
that 'it gives the stomach something else to think about!'

There are many kinds of Hangover Misery, which I basically divide into Nail-in-Brain (head type) and Tropical
Butterflies (stomach type); some unfortunates suffer both
simultaneously.

Of course, you may sagely say that anyone with the a.m.
Willies deserves everything that's coming to him (her), but
isn't that a pretty smug attitude? Didn't Oscar ('Work is the
curse of the drinking classes') Wilde say, 'Nothing succeeds
like excess'? The *occasional* excess never did anyone harm; one
might say it's essential, so that one can truly appreciate the
merits of moderation!

'Water, taken in moderation, cannot hurt anybody.'
   Mark Twain

CHAPTER 18

Miscellany

Some Other Drinks

THERE are some other well-known drinks that do not fall into any particular category but cannot be ignored. Of these the most celebrated is indubitably PIMM'S. For the record, their Cups are as follows: No. 1 – Gin; No. 2 – Whisky; No. 3 – Brandy; No. 4 – Rum; No. 5 – Rye; and No. 6 – Vodka. In each instance, only the best spirit is used from leading distillers, No. 1, The Original Gin Sling, being based on fine dry gin, not any cheaper rectified spirit.

Pimm's No. 1, by far the most popular, is subject to grave abuse, some places and people tending to doll it up into a glorified fruit salad. There is *one* way to prepare a Pimm's Gin Sling – according to the makers. It should have added to it only good quality fizzy lemonade, some ice, a slice of lemon, a little cucumber rind (or borage when available). Personally, I would add a measure of dry gin, and, if feeling extravagant, one of cointreau. It is best drunk in pints, from a glass or silver tankard. I *have* used Pimm's in a special Cocktail (see Exotica).

GINGER WINE is a very popular entirely British drink, Stone's being very widely known, though I prefer Crabbie's for a warming Whisky Mac – just half-and-half Crabbie's Green Ginger Wine and good Scotch. Do not ice it.

LIME JUICE cordial is a bar essential; there is really only one brand to consider here – Rose's. You can also obtain *unsweetened* lime juice, which is no real substitute for the fresh article; however, limes are not easily obtainable in Britain and for a Daiquiri Cocktail, it may have to be Rose's Unsweetened.

FRUIT JUICES for Cocktails should always be fresh unless a recipe actually calls for Squash. It is a mistake to economize on Squashes. There are a number of fine brands from which to choose; you get the quality you pay for. In fresh bottled juices, without preservatives, the best are certainly Britvic's. I was most impressed by a visit to their Chelmsford works.

TOMATO JUICE is another essential stand-by. Opinions vary here between Britvic, who offer a choice of formulae, and Schweppes. It is a question of taste.

A pure juice which has somewhat been neglected by Cocktail makers is APPLE, of which an excellent one is made by the Beecham group (a name guranteeing purity) and sold under the brand-name of Shloer.

Traditional BRITISH WINES – elderberry and so on – have long been a speciality of the Finsbury Distillery, and are also put out in a considerable range by the Merrydown Cider people. There is a lot of interest in Wine-making at home, and in addressing some of the energetic societies concerned with this attractive activity, I have recommended the use of very dry gin or vodka, according to type of wine, as a fortifying agent and for arresting fermentation.

One used to hear a lot about the revival of MEAD, the drink of our woad-painted remote ancestors. The only places I know where this honey-sweetened aromatic wine is regularly used are the Elizabethan Room and Star Chamber of the Gore Hotel, London. But there could be a re-revival of interest in it.

With MINERAL WATERS, Tonic and the like, go for quality, which will usually mean Sch ... though it would be ungracious not to mention the Ginger Ales of Canada Dry. (The passing of real stone ginger-beer is much to be regretted; nor can one apparently obtain a really *tart* Dry Ginger today.)

Proof (or how to bewilder the public without really trying): Nothing is more typical of archaic British practices than the Proof system as applied to drink. When it became obligatory to show the alcoholic content of all drinks was surely the opportunity to revise the method in favour of a metric one. Who, amongst consumers, can tell you what precisely is meant by the '70 proof' to be seen on most bottles of spirits? What on earth protection to the public is afforded by making it obligatory to mark the strength of drinks in a manner only an expert can interpret? But we are stuck with the system, and so is most of the Commonwealth. The USA has its own system which is nearly as complicated as the British, and just different enough to cause confusion between them. The continentals and most other countries use the perfectly logical, and therefore to us objectionable, system of giving the percentage of alcohol the drink actually contains.

We inherit our system from the days when the rough and ready way of deciding whether a spirit was up to strength was to mix it with water to the point where, when used to dampen gunpowder, the mixture would still burn explosively. Spirit of that strength was said to have been 'proved', i.e. was Proof spirit. As the science of chemistry advanced it was possible to codify this Proof Spirit as being 49·26 per cent alcohol by weight or 57·1 per cent alcohol by volume at 60 degrees Fahrenheit. Now we are approaching deep water.

Under the British Sikes system (named for the inventor of the Hydrometer used to measure it), 100 represents Proof, and absolute alcohol is presented as 175·25. However, this is theoretical as utterly pure alcohol cannot be obtained; it will always contain minute traces of water. Thus, for practical purposes, 'pure' alcohol is reckoned to be 175 Proof, which can also be expressed as 75 Over Proof. So, Whisky, etc., used commonly to be said to be '30 UP' (Under Proof) but the practice today is to say '70 per cent Proof' which is exactly the same thing. This means an alcoholic content of approximately 40 per cent by volume; the same strength being represented as 40 in the continental (Gay Lussac) system, the Germans having their own slightly different one, involving percentage of alcohol by weight instead of by volume. You will perceive we laymen are gradually getting out of our depth.

The Americans, one step ahead of the British, at least decided that Proof spirit should be an exact balance of fifty-fifty alcohol and water, and 'pure' alcohol 100 Over Proof, or, as one might express it, 200 Proof. However, this does not help much when it comes actually to indicating the strength of drinks, though it does make 70 Proof British 80 Proof American. In fact, most Scotch is exported at 86 Proof American (some higher) and American Whiskeys are customarily sold at either 90 or 100 Proof American. Got it? The round figure outline table overleaf may help, slightly. You will read about Proof Gallons from time to time, particularly when the Chancellor bangs on further additions to the fantastic imposts already levied on spirits. It means one gallon at 100 Proof; the duty payable is adjusted to this measurement, and statistics are often given in proof gallons whereas they would make more sense to you and me if they were expressed in bottles at normal strength. Simplified Table, in round figures, showing some comparison of alcoholic content and British/American/Continental equivalents for strengths of spirits:

British Proof degrees	American Proof degrees	Metric (Gay Lussac) per cent	Alcohol by Volume per cent
175	200	100	100 (pure alcohol)
100 (Proof)	114	57	57
88	100 (proof)	50	50
85	98	49	49
80	90	45	45
75	86	43	43
70	80	40	40
65	74	37	37
0	0	0	0 (water)

The more professional tables speak in terms of Under or Over Proof, but since the practice today is to use degrees Proof in labelling spirits, it seems best to follow that.

Fluid Ounce: Here's another little horror. We all have a pretty good idea what a pint, a quart or a gallon, or fraction of those, mean, and it seems extraordinary that under regulations enforced for the consumer's protection, the contents of a bottle should be stated under a form of measurement, a fluid ounce, of which he is very unlikely to have the remotest comprehension. If it said $1\frac{1}{3}$ pints we would understand, but no – a bottle of spirits (except Brandy) contains '26$\frac{2}{3}$ fl. oz.' That's what it says.

What is this strange entity, the fluid ounce? If you want the official answer, it's a measure of water weighing one standard ounce at a temperature of 62 degrees Fahrenheit and an atmospheric pressure of 30 inches. Wiser? The Americans have their own Fluid Ounce, which is one-sixteenth of a US pint. This makes the US Fluid ounce fractionally bigger than the British one, which perhaps compensates for the fact that the American gallon is smaller, there being 1·2 American gallons for each 1 British gallon. This all helps to complicate things, and also leads to trouble bottle-wise. When an American refers to a 'Quart' of spirits he means a bottle of 33·3 British fluid ounces, and by a 'Fifth' (of a gallon) he means a bottle holding exactly the same as a Scotch bottle with us, whereas British standard spirit bottles run at six to the imperial gallon and, to add further confusion, hold a 'reputed quart', not a true quart, which would mean a bottle held a quarter, not a sixth, of a gallon. (We are now using the 40 oz. bottle – 1 true (Imperial) Quart – quite a lot in Britain). I would add that the American and British proof gallons naturally differ and neither should be confused with the Liquid gallon. Had enough? (In recipes I express quantity measures in terms of fluid ounces – just called 'oz'. – because 1 and/or 2 oz. measures are easily obtainable).

'*Out*': UK licensed premises must state they are using a '6-Out' measure or optic; or a '5-Out' or a rare '4'. This refers to the capacity of the measure in terms of the gill (4 gills; 1 pint). Thus, a '6-Out' indicates that six of them make up a gill. This is the most common measure in England, the Scottish preferring the more generous '5-Out' (or 1 fluid ounce). The '4-Out' is sometimes called a Club measure and is the largest in normal use in Britain. One used to find thieving '7-Outs' which at the time of writing are about to become illegal.

I now list alphabetically a few further oddments of information not totally without relevance to this book.

'*Appellation Contrôlée*': If you see this on a wine bottle under *Chablis, Beaune*, etc., it is some guarantee that the wine comes from the district involved and on French-bottled wines is hedged by strict laws. But outside France and a few other European wine-producing countries, there is no protection for generic names for French wines (Burgundy etc.) except champagne – now protected in England – and, of course, famous trade names (*chateaux* and firms).

Bond: A store under control of the Customs authorities, where alcoholic beverages may be kept Duty Free. The excise duty is paid when liquor is removed: it then becomes Duty Paid.

Booze: I don't think many have any idea of the origin of this word which is often used and which certainly is the slang term for our subject. Oscar Mendelsohn suggests a connexion with *boozah*, a very ancient Egyptian brew, through the Middle English *bousen* (to drink deeply), but another authority says it comes from an old falconry term, *bowze*, describing the action of a bird drinking; a constant dipping of the head to the liquid.

Bottles (*outsize*): In commerce you do not ordinarily find bottles above a Magnum (2 bottles) but I have found myself arguing about the larger sizes which exist. Contents are not necessarily precise, nor is the origin of the Biblical names known: By Bottles – Jeroboam (Double Magnum; occasionally found on lists, particularly with champagne) – 4; Rehoboam – 6; Methuselah – 8; Salamanazar – 12; Balthazar – 16; Nebuchanezzar – 20. Wine does keep longer in larger bottles.

Case: 12 bottles. A 'mixed case' (such as are often advertised around Christmas) means 12 bottles of various spirits, wines, etc.

Cold: It is *not* a good idea to have strong drinks before going *out* into cold weather. In fact, if cold and alcohol be excessive, one may crumble to the ground. The apparent warming action of spirits on coming *in* from the cold is illusory though stimulating: alcohol actually reduces body temperature.

Lemons: One should at all costs try to obtain lemons *without preservatives;* even after washing, the normal fruit of commerce can taint, say, a Dry Martini.

'Liqueur': The origin of this word, indiscriminately applied to fine spirits of all sorts as well as to such drinks as Cointreau, is *liqueur de dessert*, meaning in French a sweet drink taken with the dessert course.

Metric Measures (round figure equivalents): 1 litre – 1·7 pints; 1 (Br.) Gallon – 4·5 litres; 1 pint – ·56 litre; 5 litres – 1·1 gallons.

'Pétillant': A word sometimes used without knowledge: French to describe a slightly effervescent wine, as opposed to a fully 'sparkling' one. Could be applied to many of the Portuguese table wines now becoming popular in Britain.

Pink Champagne (*'Champagne Rosé'*): A fad which seems to come in cycles. It is produced simply by the addition of a little red wine during production.

Sophisticated: You may think you are, but if you use this in sophisticated circles you may find they take it in its old sense, for vinously it means adulterated.

Strenghts (approximate average alcoholic content by volume per cent): Gin, Scotch, Brandy, Rum – 40; Vodka – 37; table wines – 10; Sherry, Port – 18; Champagne – 12; Vermouth – 18; liqueurs (and ciders) – vary greatly.

Teetotal: Probably of American origin (it's hard to know whether the USA has suffered more from Prohibitionists or from Alcohol) denoting *Total Temperance*, as opposed to semi-temperance involving abstention only from spirits. Strictly, Temperance only means moderation but has come to be synonymous with total abstinence and/or Prohibition.

Toast: Drinking to someone's health is an age-old and international habit, and today ranges from the formal Loyal Toast at banquets (and subsequent Toasts prefaced by speeches amusing or yawn-provoking) to the casual salutations 'Cheers', '*à la vôtre*', '*Skoll*', '*Prosit*', '*Salud*', or whatever. The origin of the word 'Toast' is obscure, but would seem to come from what we eat for breakfast. In Elizabethan times scorched bread (probably spiced) was put into wines. In the 17th century the word became associated with a person, usually an attractive lady – hence 'Toast of the Town' for a reigning beauty – but later gained wider meaning.

Tobacco: It is pleasing to smoke a cigar with one's coffee and liqueur, but abstention from tobacco during a heavy evening's celebration will considerably reduce the prospect of 'parrot's-cage mouth' and other morning-after symptoms.

> 'What harm in drinking can there be,
> Since punch and life so well agree.'
>
> *Thos. Blacklock*

CHAPTER 19

A Bar of One's Own – Let's Give a Cocktail Party

WHILE it is not an inexpensive hobby, a Bar at home can provide a lot of fun. It is, indeed, something of a status symbol to have a Bar (rather than just a Cocktail cabinet) and if you are lucky enough to have the space, I suggest setting aside a separate room for it. If not, one's bar should be part of the sitting-room, not the sitting-room part of the bar – as I know has happened in the home of an acquaintance of mine. It is rather like living in a pub, attractive to some men but not every woman's dream-house!

Basic bar equipment need not be costly or elaborate. You require a cocktail shaker, and I recommend the standard type. The two piece Boston shaker, requiring a separate strainer, is for professionals or experts. You also require a mixing-glass, with a lip for easy pouring, and a strainer. By far the best strainers are the traditional ones with a springy wire edge. If you can find metal bar equipment in stainless steel, you will save on polishing. A long bar spoon and a measure – and you are in business. A one-ounce ('5-Out') measure is adequate, but you may find a double one – measuring a 'single' one side and a 'double' when reversed – is convenient. A separate bowl for pouring off melted ice from the shaker and an ice-bowl are valuable.

For glasses, I would not get too small cocktail-glasses, as it is best not to fill them completely: that makes for spillage. Tall glasses are needed for 'long' drinks. Don't forget a good corkscrew and robust bottle and can opener, again preferably stainless.

From these beginnings you can build up with all sorts of amusing, useful, senseless, costly, gadgets. If you win the Pools have a look at Asprey's in Bond Street and Fortnum and Mason's in Piccadilly, but, failing that, most department stores have a wide range of cocktail accessories. Avoid over-ornate, gilded utensils; they are not very 'professional'.

Take a fresh look at Cocktail Bars in hotels you know or happen to visit: you will pick up good ideas. And do talk to bartenders. By their profession they meet a terrible lot of bores, but I haven't encountered a good bartender yet who wasn't happy to discuss bar equipment, mixed drinks and the like. Don't most of us enjoy talking about *our* job? You will get some interesting hints this way.

Your Bar itself can be do-it-yourself or you can buy the complete article. If making your own, top it with Formica, or, for the ingenious, marble recovered from grandma's wash-stand, which will provide a good working surface and will not be stained by alcohol rings which tends to happen with wood. A lot of people like to decorate their bars with advertising materials from the major firms, who will usually send signs, ashtrays and the like to individuals. Ideally, a bar will have its own fridge or ice-maker.

As for stock, your basic requirements are good dry Gin, Scotch, Brandy, Vermouths sweet and dry, Angostura bitters, Cointreau, Grenadine syrup, Lime and fruit juices, and mineral waters. Keep lemons and oranges to hand. A Sparklet soda-water maker is valuable as a stand-by, though for perfection I prefer Sch ... bottled soda. But if you get the Cocktail habit, you'll quickly find you require a lot of other liquors; half, or smaller, bottles will do for those of which you use only a little at a time, such as expensive liqueurs, or infrequently used cordials. You will probably quickly develop bottle-mania, collecting different liquors as others collect books. At that stage, you will soon be giving *me* advice.

LET'S GIVE A COCKTAIL PARTY

You don't need a bar in order to give a Cocktail Party, though if you do have a bar you are bound to. You can either mix the drinks in the kitchen and bring them in on trays or set aside a table for the mixing. You may, of course, decide to hire a bartender and have the event catered for, but here I am speaking about doing it all yourself.

Decide on a basic one or two Cocktails, say a dry one and a sweet one, or a Cocktail plus a Cup or Punch. There is nothing wrong in preparing these a little in advance and storing them in a refrigerator, though you may prefer to mix them in front of your guests.

One thing you will need is more ice than any normal household can provide: in plenty of time, order some from your fishmonger, and rinse it well. To break it up, you need a sharp pick. Then, if you wrap the pieces in a clean cloth and give them a bashing on a hard surface, you will have lumps of convenient size. This will be good 'hard' commercial ice which stays frozen longer than that from a domestic fridge. If set out in an ice bucket for use in Cocktail-making or by guests, a splash of soda-water over it prevents the lumps sticking together as if cemented.

Glasses you will either own, or in many instances off-licence stores lend them free against payments for breakages: but they expect the order for your drinks. (You may occasionally have to pay a small charge). It is also probable that your off-licence will provide your drink requirements on a sale-or-return basis – you are credited for any untouched bottles you send back. This allows you to be well stocked: there is nothing more humiliating than running out of booze.

Send out your invitations well in advance. These can range from an extravagant engraved personalized gold-edged card to a simple do-it-yourself hand-written invitation. I suggest a card of elegant (non-gimmicky) form which you can buy at any decent stationers. Get one clearly marked RSVP (or definitely requesting a reply) and the probability is most people will let you know if they are coming. It is a great convenience to host and hostess to know this.

All this may seem pretty obvious stuff to some, but I assure you a great many people who regularly entertain at home neglect certain elementary rules – and wonder why their parties don't succeed completely.

Remember, I am writing here about a Cocktail Party – not an evening reception nor a casual week-end get-together – but a Cocktail Party, an event demanding a certain minimal etiquette. It is worth a little extra trouble.

More Points to Remember

Do not try to get in more people than your room(s) will comfortably hold. Remove your more frangible ornaments or put them out of reach. Set out every ashtray you can find, beg or buy. Adequately cover polished wood surfaces, or put out drip-mats – they may even be used.

Children, unless precociously well-behaved, are not an adornment at these essentially adult events. State the timing of your party with firm grace: e.g. 6 to 8 p.m. You will then be indicating something when you start those meaningful looks at the clock at 8.15.

You are not expected to *feed* your guests at the Cocktail Party: a few may be staying on to eat with you, by special invitation, but your Cocktail Party is a prelude to watching telly, dining-out, going to the cinema, having a row, or whatever it is your guests do on, I suggest, Friday evening: it is not a nosh-up. Friday is usually an excellent day for a party, a good run down to the week-end, though I know people who choose Mondays as they reckon it brightens the beginning of the week.

You will need to provide some small snacks. The lazy, expensive way is to buy these in a delicatessen. In place of the usual canapés – which I have elsewhere described as 'scraps of offal on soggy toast' – I prefer the following simple, easily-prepared 'eats': really spicy little sausages; plain whole green olives; a good paté on crisp little biscuits; home-made cheese straws; cubes of New Zealand cheddar: there is an infinite variety of nibbles one can dream up or get from books. Simplicity is the thing to go for: and nothing that needs more than two bites at the most. Place 'eats' around so those that want to can help themselves: don't lunge at your guests with possibly unwanted nourishment.

Assuming, like me, you use no hired help, tip off a few special pals to stand by to pass round trays of drinks. Whatever basic Cocktail and/or Punch you are serving, have Scotch whisky, gin and a medium-dry sherry available for those who only drink this. Do not forget the non-drinkers, and have plenty of mineral waters to hand. Place cigarettes (tipped and plain) at strategic points, and a thoughtful host might provide some of those small mild cigars that are increasingly popular.

Neither over-light the room nor try to romanticize the scene by turning off all but a few lamps. Obscurity belongs to discothêques, not drawing-rooms. In lighting, your consideration should be to provide a flattering illumination for the women present. Candles are not only decorative, but help to disperse cigarette smoke. Remember, a room-full of people warms up with surprising speed: even on a cold evening you may have to turn off heating. Try to achieve good ventilation without draughts. Background music must be *in* the background: this is no occasion for giving a recital of your newest LPs. Dancing does not take place at Cocktail Parties, and on no account set aside a room for showing your latest home movies. We are writing of a fairly formal, if gay, event with carefully selected guests who will enjoy conversation and sophisticated refreshment.

Be mindful of those you know to be driving when they leave you and do not press on them that most fatal of all British drinks, One For The Road. *He who encourages a driver to drink too much is as culpable as the driver who accepts more than his reasonable quota.*

'Many a man who thinks to found a home discovers that he has merely opened a tavern for his friends.'

N. Douglas

CHAPTER 20

Exotica – Just For Fun

WHILE some of these drinks are palatable, they have no serious place in the instructive and broadly sensible recipes appended to appropriate chapters. It would mainly take very highly-stocked bars to provide the ingredients; yet they are rather fun – if only to read – and the most dedicated Cocktail-men must be allowed moments of frivolity. So here goes:

1. Cock Ale

Since we have heard so much of Cocktails, perhaps you'd be amused by a recipe for 'Cock Ale', dating from 1736: 'To make Cock Ale, take ten gallons of ale and a large cock, the larger the better. Parboil the cock, flea him and stamp him in a stone mortar until his bones are broken. You must craw and gut him when you flea [skin] him. Put him into two quarts of sack [sherry] and put to it three pounds of raisins of the sun stoned, some blades of mace and a few cloves. Put all these into a canvas bag and a little while before you find the ale has done working, put the ale and bag together into a vessel. In a week or nine days time bottle it up, fill the bottles but just above the necks and leave the same to ripen as other ale.'

I like the word 'ripen'!

2. Gipsy's Brew

A Romany specific against arthritis.

1 Pint 'Booth's' Gin
1 Quart Strong Ale
2 6-inch roots of Horseradish (gathered in Spring)
    Mix Gin and Ale; grate in horseradish.
    Leave standing for 3 days in open vessel.
    Strain and bottle.
    Dose: small wine-glass nightly.
     Miss Mabel Brown

3. Pousse Café

This oddity has come to mean liqueurs expertly layered in a tall thin glass so that they remain separated. It is a question of specific gravity, though, as a drink, a matter for levity. This sort of thing was once taken quite seriously and it was averred that whatever the ingredients they should always be odd in number. Here is Rainbow Pousse Café, just for the record. In exactly equal amounts, over the back of a spoon, pour

Crème de Càcao
Crème de Violette
Yellow Chartreuse
Maraschino
Benedictine
Green Chartreuse
Cognac
   UKBG

Strictly an 'our-next-trick-is-impossible' business.

4. Red Lion Punch

(Based on an 18th-century recipe from Oxford which was much more complicated.)

Extract the Juice from the rind of 3 Fresh (washed) Lemons by rubbing them with Lump Sugar. Discard rinds, retaining Flavoured Sugar.

Cut the peel very thinly from 2 Oranges and 2 Lemons.

Press the Juice from 4 Oranges and 10 Lemons.

Take 6 wine-glasses of Calves-Foot Jelly in liquid state. Stir the above, including the Sugar, in a very large jug or other suitable container. Pour on top 4 pints of boiling water. Stir mixture and place close to (but not on) a fire for $\frac{3}{4}$-hour.

Strain carefully into another large container. Sweeten with $1\frac{1}{2}$ pints of Syrup made by boiling $1\frac{1}{4}$ lb. Sugar in $1\frac{1}{4}$ pints water (to which with advantage a wine-glass of Orange Curaçao may then be added).

Add 2 bottles of Booth's Gin and 1 bottle of Medium-Dry White Wine. Bottle in suitable containers and store under refrigeration (the addition of ice to the punch itself is not recommended). Or may be served hot (do not boil).

5. Toledo Punch

(This was invented by Harry Johnson in the Middle West, getting on for a century ago, and his recipe reflects a more spacious age.)

In a huge bowl place 2 lb. Sugar and mix in 4 large bottles Soda-Water, Juice of 4 Lemons, 4 oz. Cognac, 4 Oranges and a Pineapple cut up, Grapes and Strawberries if available. Add
6 bottles quality Champagne
$\frac{1}{2}$ bottle Cognac
2 bottles Good Claret
4 large bottles of natural sparkling Mineral Water (Appolinaris)

Mix well together and refrigerate.
Serve in glasses suitably dressed with Fruits.

6. V.I.P.

(Evolved by the author for the film of the same name starring Elizabeth Taylor and Richard Burton)

$1\frac{1}{2}$ oz. 'High & Dry' Gin

1 oz. Pimms No. 1

2 oz. Passion Fruit Juice

$\frac{1}{2}$ oz. Martini Dry Vermouth

$\frac{1}{2}$ oz. Fresh Lemon Juice

Shake vigorously and strain into adequate goblet. Decorate with White Water Lotus Nut impaled on Cocktail-stick.

7. Zombie

$\frac{3}{4}$ oz. Unsweetened Pineapple Juice

$\frac{3}{4}$ oz. Papaya Juice (canned)

Juice of a Large Lime

$\frac{3}{4}$ oz. Powdered Sugar

$\frac{3}{4}$ oz. Apricot Brandy

1 oz. Heavy Dark Rum (90 proof)

2 oz. Dark Rum

Shake well with cracked ice and pour entire contents without straining into tall frosted glass (a Zombie glass). Add ice to fill. Decorate with Mint sprig, and cube of Pineapple and Cherry suspended over drink on stick.

Float on top dash of 150 proof tropical Rum. Sprinkle Powdered Sugar on top, and serve with straws.

Mr Eddie Clarke

(Don't ask me where you get 150 proof Rum.)

'The rapturous, wild and ineffable pleasure of drinking at somebody else's expense.'

H. S. Leigh

Envoi and Apologia

WITHIN the scope of a slim volume I have ambitiously tried to cover quite a lot of ground. I hope some have learned a little, and that those who have learned nothing new have at least found some stimulus to thought. Inevitably there are omissions; great names receive scant acclaim, or nil; whole areas in potables are neglected. The treatment of some subjects is sketchy: that reflects the lacunae in my own knowledge for, to repeat, this is one man's book – not a symposium – and can contain only what I know and expose what I do not, must involve my own prejudices and preferences. Yet I believe it carries out its expressed intentions, within the limits set, to be neither definitive reference nor purely light entertainment, to instruct and, I sincerely trust, rarely to bore: if I have succeeded only in the last condition I shall rest content.

J.D.

'An expert is one who knows more and more about less and less.'

N. B. Butler

Acknowledgements

BIBLIOGRAPHY – Books and Other Publications:

AN ANTHOLOGY OF COCKTAILS – Booth's Distilleries,
   London (private printing)
THE A–Z PARTY BOOK – *Daily Mirror*, 1963
THE BARKEEPER'S GOLDEN BOOK – O. Blunier (Mort-
   garten-Verlag Ag., Zurich, 1935)
BARTENDER'S GUIDE – Trader Vic (Garden City Books,
   New York, 1948. $3·95)
BARTENDER'S MANUAL – Harry Johnson, New York
   (published by the author, 1900 edition)
THE BOOK OF UNUSUAL QUOTATIONS (Cassell and Co.,
   London)
THE BOOK OF VODKA – John Bradley Hutton (J. and J.
   Vickers and Co. Ltd, London)
CASSELL'S CLASSIFIED QUOTATIONS
CHAMBER'S ENCYCLOPAEDIA (various editions)
THE DICTIONARY OF DRINK AND DRINKING – Oscar A.
   Mendelsohn (Macmillan, 1965, 45s.)
DICTIONARY OF WINES, SPIRITS & LIQUEURS – André
   Simon (Herbert Jenkins, London, 1961. 21s.)
ENCYCLOPAEDIA AMERICANA
ENCYCLOPAEDIA BRITANNICA (11th edition, et. seq.)
THE FINE ART OF MIXING DRINKS – David A. Embury
   (Faber and Faber, London. 30s. new revised edition)

GUIDE TO WINES AND SPIRITS – edited by Ralph Churchill (*Licensed Victuallers' Gazette and Off-Licence Journal*, London)

INTERNATIONAL GUIDE TO DRINKS–The United Kingdom Bartenders' Guild (1960 and 1965 editions)

THE KINDRED SPIRIT (A History of Gin and the House of Booth) – Lord Kinross (with H. K. Humphreys) (Newman Neame Ltd, 21s. 1959)

KING COCKTAIL – Eddie Clarke (private printing, 7s. 6d.)

KNOWING ALCOHOLIC BEVERAGES – 1965, reprinted from *Liquor Store* Magazine (Jobson Publishing Corp., New York City, $1)

MISCELLANY OF CURIOUS AND AMUSING FACTS – Boord and Son, London (limited private edition 1894)

THE OXFORD ENGLISH DICTIONARY

THE PAN BOOK OF WINE – articles from House and Garden, 1964. (Pan Books, 3s. 6d.)

PROFESSIONAL MIXING GUIDE – Dr J. G. B. Siegert and Sons (Angostura bitters)

RIDLEY'S WINE AND SPIRIT HANDBOOK (1965. Ridley's Ltd, London)

SAVOY COCKTAIL BOOK – Savoy Hotel Ltd, London. 1965 edition. (Constable and Co, 21s.)

SCOTCH WHISKY – Questions and Answers (The Scotch Whisky Association, Edinburgh)

SHAKING IN THE 60s – Eddie Clarke (Cocktail Books Ltd, 23 Albemarle Street, London, W.1. 25s.)

THE STORY OF GIN – David Jermyn (Booth's Distilleries Ltd, London)

THE STORY OF IRISH WHISKEY –(Irish Whiskey Association, Dublin)

THE TREASURY OF HUMOROUS QUOTATIONS – Nicholas Bentley and Evan Eskar (J. M. Dent and Sons, 5s.)

Booth's Handbook of Cocktails and Mixed Drinks

THE TRUE DRUNKARD'S DELIGHT – William Juniper
   (Unicorn Press, London, 1933. Limited edition)
WINES AND SPIRITS – L. W. Marrison (Penguin Books.
   Revised edition, 1965)

FURTHER ACKNOWLEDGEMENTS – magazines,
   companies, organizations and individuals:

Mr Denzil Batchelor
Beecham Group (Food Division)
Mr Roy Blunt
Bourbon Institute, New York City
Carl Byoir and Associates, London
Capital Wine Agencies Ltd
Canada Dry Ltd
Casa de Portugal, London
Charrington United Breweries Ltd
Coates and Co., Plymouth
Cointreau Information Centre (C.S. Service Ltd, London)
John Crabbie and Company, Leith
Daily Telegraph (week-end magazine, 10 December, 1965)
Davis, Hammond and Barton Ltd, London
The Distillers Company Ltd
Everywoman Magazine (party leaflet)
Grants of St James's Ltd
John Haig and Co. Ltd
Harper's Magazine (December, 1949)
Harveys of Bristol
International Beverage News (December 1965 et seq.)
Herbert Jenkins, London (Cocktail Key. 2s.)
Mr George Marshall
Martini and Rossi Ltd (London)

Matthew Clark and Sons Ltd
Pimms Ltd, London
Mr Cyril Ray
Edouard Robinson Ltd, London
Rose Kia-Ora Sales Co. Ltd, London
Schweppes Ltd
House of Seagram, London
South African Wine Farmers Association (London)
Tanqueray Gordon and Co. Ltd, London
United Rum Merchants Ltd, London
John Walker and Sons Ltd
Mr Ross Wilson
Wine and Food (Spring edition, 1965)
Ted Worner Associates, New York City

Index

185

Index

H. E. Bravery

THE COMPLETE BOOK OF
HOME WINE-MAKING   40p

This unique book contains something for
everybody. The recipes are new and economical, but thoroughly tried and tested.

The methods are simply explained and easy to
follow.

'The truth is that well-made home-made wine,
made with a good recipe and method and a bit of
common sense is as good and often better than
commercial products ... put your mind to it
and you will make wines the like of which you
always thought were beyond you' – from the
author's Introduction.

These and other PAN Books are obtainable
from all booksellers and newsagents. If you
have any difficulty please send purchase price
plus 7p postage to PO Box 11, Falmouth,
Cornwall.
While every effort is made to keep prices low,
it is sometimes necessary to increase prices at
short notice. PAN Books reserve the right to
show new retail prices on covers which may
differ from those advertised in the text or
elsewhere.

BOOTH'S HANDBOOK
of
COCKTAILS
and
MIXED DRINKS

Spirits – Aperitifs – Liqueurs – Cordials – Wines –
Beers – Ciders – Cocktails – 'Mocktails' – Cups –
Punches – Hangovers – Bars – Pubs – Parties – Facts
– Fallacies – Opinions – Curiosities – Novelties –
Advice – Entertainment – Recipes . . .